In the early sixties a lifestyle evolved for young people that was mysterious, exciting and fast-moving. It was directed from within and needed no justification from without. Kids were clothes-obsessed, cool, dedicated to R&B and their own dances.
They called themselves 'Mods'.

For the late Pete Meaden

Mods!

Compiled by Richard Barnes

Plexus, London

Copyright © 1979 by Richard Barnes
Published by Plexus Publishing Ltd
26 Dafforne Road
London SW17 8TZ

This book was originally published
by Eel Pie Publishing Ltd in 1979
This edition published by
Plexus Publishing Ltd in 1991

British Library Cataloguing in Publication data

Barnes, Richard, 1944 Oct. 3.
　Mods! – 5th ed.
　781.66

ISBN 0 85965 173 8

Compiled and designed by Richard Barnes

Richard Barnes would like to thank Johnny Moke and Jan
McVeigh for their assistance in compiling this book.

A large proportion of the photographs included in this
book were taken in 1964 by Terence Spencer (Colorific
Photo Library).

Many thanks to the following for their assistance: The
Hairdressers Journal, FAB/208 magazine (formerly Fabulous
magazine), Clarks Shoes, Martyn Atkins, Ian Wright, Lin
Gibson, Ric Cunningham, Jack English, Contemporary
Wardrobe, Roy Carr, Keith Altham (formerly Fab's Keith),
Willie Deasey.

Printed in Great Britain by The Bath Press

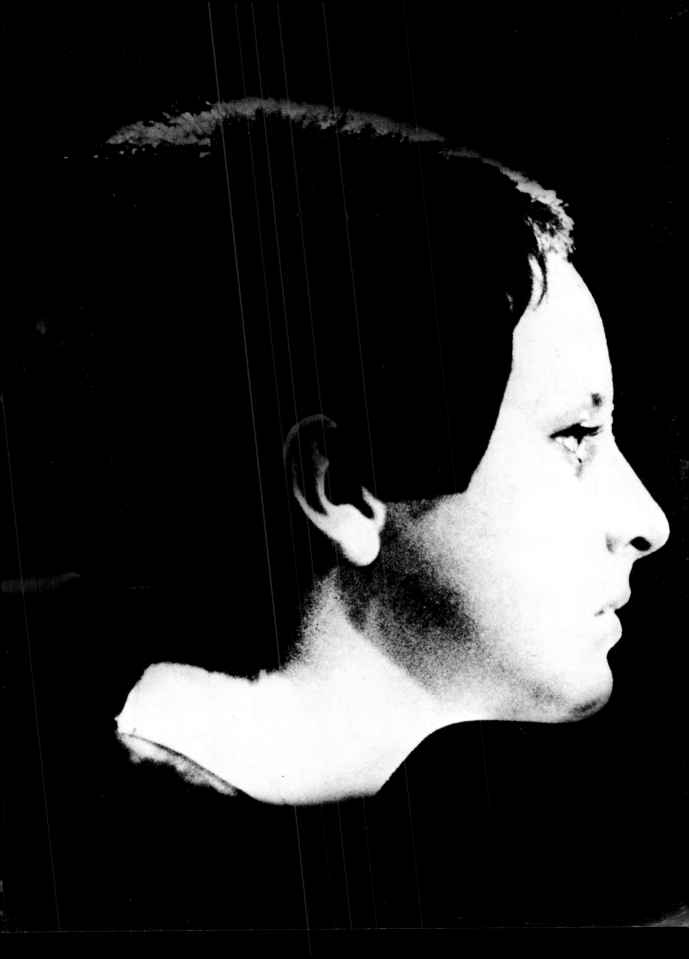

We'd just come out from the Scene to cool down a bit. It was incredibly hot and sweaty down there and we were doing the next most-cool thing, which was to hang around in Ham Yard and check each other out. The Scene club used to get pretty humid and their ventilation system consisted of a brick to hold the door open. When you first arrived, though, it was usually freezing. A lot of kids were standing around in Ham Yard in small groups talking. Half of them were pilled-up. Pete Meaden had taken about six 'blues' and was talking at everyone and clicking his fingers West Side Story-style.

It was one of those odd moments in life which you know you will remember sometime in the future. I knew that night that I would actually look back on it in years to come. It wasn't a particularly memorable night. It was exciting at the Scene club, it usually was. There were lots of interesting new people and the D.J., Guy Stevens, the man with the best R & B record collection in the country, was playing some of his precious rare records. But I think what was memorable and struck me most that night, was that I fully realised that there existed a complete Mod way of life. I'd been involved with Mods and Mod fashions and music and been carried along by it all, but that night it hit me how all-embracing the lifestyle was, and how committed and intense everyone was about it.

I wasn't a Mod and never even thought of being a Mod. I was at Art School. My involvement with Mods came because my friend from Art School, with whom I shared a flat, played in a group which had recently come under the co-management of Pete Meaden, and Pete Meaden, lived, ate and slept Mod. He was in the process of masterminding the group into a Mod group. I was very involved with them and so saw and experienced much of what they did at that time. Also I ran an R & B club with a friend which eventually turned into a Mod's stronghold.

The Mod way of life consisted of total devotion to looking and being 'cool'. Spending practically all your money on clothes and all your after work hours in clubs and dance halls. To be part-time was really to miss the point. It was all very new and fast and to me a bit mysterious.

The Scene wasn't licensed and only sold orange juice. It wasn't considered particularly cool to smoke or drink anyway, but we wanted a drink. So a group of us made our way down through the Soho evening crowds of Windmill Street to a pub. Mods had their own style of walking. They swayed their shoulders and took short steps, with their feet slightly turned out. It was more of a swagger, a walk of confidence. They'd sometimes have their hands held together behind their backs under their coats or plastic macs and these would sway as they bowled along. If their hands were in their pockets they would have their thumbs sticking out. That was the look. This particular night I noticed both Pete Meaden and Pete Townshend had the walk off to a T.

The small group of us swaggered into the pub. You either drank scotch and coke, vodka and lime or an orange juice. Mickey Tenner and Pete Meaden and somebody else were talking at each other so much that they never touched their drinks, although Meaden constantly picked up his scotch and coke and let it hover near his lips for a few thousand words and put it down again.

After a while Pete and I left Meaden, Mickey Tenner and the others and strolled around by Shaftesbury Avenue talking about Mods and the lifestyle. We'd been overwhelmed by Pete Meaden when we first met him. He was English but talked like an American radio disc jockey, really fast and slick. He called everybody 'Baby!' 'Hey, how are you Peter Baby, too much, what's happening, great, keep cool, can you dig it? Barney Baybee, s'nice to see you again, O.K. Baby?'

I'd never heard Murray the K or other fast talking Americans. Meaden never stopped for breath. He was like somebody you'd see in films, only he was this side of the screen, standing in front of you. He was bursting with ideas and energy and had great plans to turn the group into a cult phenomenon. The group had just got a new manager, a businessman who had a foundry that made door handles and castings in Shepherds Bush. I thought he had the idea that any businessman with the money could be a Brian Epstein. After all, managing a pop group must have seemed a lot easier than working for a fortune. Pete Meaden was hired as a publicist. We had changed their name a few months before, but he changed it once again. They were to be called the 'High Numbers'. All very Mod and esoteric. There was a lot of talk about 'Image' and 'Direction'. He was going to try to establish the group in the most important Soho Mod clubs. Meaden didn't have a lot of money, he did a bit of publicity for various pop groups for which he was poorly paid, but somehow he always looked sharp and immaculate. Quite often he would appear in a different new-looking jacket and smart trousers although he only lived in his tiny office in Monmouth Street which just had a chair, a telephone, a sleeping bag, a filing cabinet and an ironing board. He knew what was 'in' and where to get it.

This particular evening Pete and I were discussing the very point of what was 'in' and why. Meaden and Mickey Tenner and some others in the Scene club had been saying that it was time to stop wearing something or other and that such and such would be very 'hip' next week. It was incredible to me that the fashions were constantly changing, and the frequency with which they did. I wondered who thought them up. I was convinced that there was an inner clique of policy-making Mods who dictated fashion. I wondered whether they had a secret bunker beneath the Scene club, and whether Pete Meaden wasn't one of them. Now, looking back, as I knew that night I would, I realise how naïve my suspicions were. However, wrong as I was, I had touched on what I suspect was a fundamental ingredient of the whole Sixties Mod thing.

I had assumed that there was a group of self-appointed Mod leaders who controlled the direction of the rest of the Mods. What I had never assumed was that the Mod 'movement' was controlled by business-men, middle-aged plastic D.J.'s, music publishers, the CIA or the media. That's because it wasn't. The very idea, again, is to miss the point. Their entire look came from within their own undefined ranks. Apart from one or two individual journalists, the press didn't have a clue as to what was happening until the Bank Holiday riots in 1964. Up to then they weren't particularly interested anyway. The whole thing was far too mysterious for them to find it very newsworthy.

Mods were first and foremost concerned with their looks. They were obsessed with clothes and with being cool at all times. What happened outside their world of clothes shops, coffee bars, street corners, dance halls and clubs didn't concern them greatly. If the press did pick up on a certain aspect of their world, the kids more than likely dropped it. They were rela-tively affluent and determined to spend all their money and every moment of their spare time on their leisure. The days belonged to society, to the boss, to others, but when they got home from work, washed, changed, and went out, the nights and weekends belonged to them. To understand how new it all was, it is necessary to understand how young and exciting the sixties were. After the forties and fifties, it seemed like England had taken its stays off and discovered how free and alive life could be. Also, to understand how Mods began, it is necessary to understand something of the only other young people previously to have established their own identity — the Teddy Boys.

Before the fifties, teenagers didn't exist as a separate consumer group. They were classed as either children or adults. By the early fifties school leavers were earning better wages. As they didn't have any responsibilities other than giving Mum something towards their keep, they had a lot to spend. However there wasn't a market catering specifically for them. They bought the same clothes, saw the same films, listened to the same radio programmes, watched the same T.V. and listened to the same popular music as their parents.

Popular music at that time was particularly dire. I've always thought that if ever there was a cause for the vandalism of the Teddy boys, it wasn't Bill Haley's music but the sugary pap churned out by the music industry of the fifties and the B.B.C. light programme. B.B.C. radio played exactly what Tin Pan Alley wanted under an agreement they had which was in operation right up to the middle of the fifties. In those days the big money was in selling sheet music rather than records. Anyone who thinks the Eurovision song contest is bad and doesn't remember the fifties should take a listen to this selection of typical early fifties hits. *Hot Diggity, Pickin' a Chicken, Bushel and a Peck, Gilly*

Gilly Ossenfeffer Katzenellen Bogen By the Sea, Happy Wanderer, Close the Door (They're Coming Through the Window), Oh Mein Papa, Where will the Baby's Dimple Be?, Sugarbush, Twenty Tiny Fingers and *I See The Moon (The Moon Sees Me).*

It didn't take too long for these young people to latch onto music that they could call theirs and that the older generation didn't like. They rejected the muzak for the 'proles' which the radio played, and took to American Rock 'n Roll. This craze grew and grew. Soon there was a booming teenage market as business-men realised the kids had a lot of money and nothing to spend it on. They adopted and adapted the Edwardian look and the press named them Teddy Boys. All of a sudden teenagers were discovered, and soon after this 'juvenile delinquency' arrived.

A lot changed in the fifties. Britain thought it was the most important and powerful nation after the U.S.A. and U.S.S.R. It rigidly stuck to the idea that 'British was Best' and unbeatable. It was a time of complacency and head-in-the-sand burying. We still led the world in all sorts of things, like motor cycles. We had Lord Docker, the head of B.S.A., showing off his Rolls Royce and wife's furs to prove it. We sent our Army to Suez to put the Egyptians in their place but the blighters kicked us out. Hundreds of thousands of people marched from Aldermaston, to protest about the hydrogen bomb.

For the kids, the two most important things were that compulsory call-up into the army for boys of 18 was abolished, and that hire purchase was introduced. This made it easy to buy a portable *Dansette* record player, (gramaphone to parents), to play the new smaller, more convenient records that had been introduced, which played at 45 r.p.m.

The working class could afford cars, television sets and washing machines. It was the time of the 'I'm-alright-Jack' and 'You've-never-had-it-so-Good' materialism of Harold Macmillan's consumer boom. The attitude was 'Live Now, Pay Later'. (When you think about it, they did — and we are).

Lonnie Donnegan started a craze for skiffle music that swept the country and had thousands of kids playing it in makeshift groups. If it hadn't been for skiffle bringing music-making into the bedrooms and sheds of so many British homes, it's unlikely that British rock would have become the most important in the world in the sixties.

Home grown Rock 'n Roll stars emerged in the latter part of the fifties. The biggest were Cliff Richard, Billy Fury and Adam Faith. I often wondered why some were so strangely named, like Marty Wilde, Vince Eager, Billy Fury, Cuddly Duddley, Dickie Pride, Duffy Power and Johnny Gentle, who were all handled by Larry Parnes. Larry Parnes was the archetypal publicity-conscious music-biz manager.

The Teddy Boys had got very violent and moronic and ripped up cinema seats with cut-throat razors. The 'look' had spread all over the country, but then it died out. Drape jackets and brothel creepers were very dated by about 1958. At this time the Italian look came in for teenagers. Italian suits had short box jackets and narrow trousers with no turn-ups, and were worn with winklepicker shoes. The jackets were so short they were named 'bumfreezer' jackets. They had two or three buttons and very narrow lapels. If they were double-breasted the crossover was only about 2 inches. It was this look that the early originators of the Mods took to and developed.

The Teddy Boys had broken new ground. They had established a teenage market. They had introduced a fashion that was totally working class in its origins. And they had made it acceptable for males to dress purely for show. Before that, working class men either dressed for work, or had a 'Sunday Best' suit that was made to last for about twenty years. Casual clothes, either American or Continental, were unavailable and the boring stuff that existed in England was aimed at the upper class older market.

The second and most important manifestation of adolescent fashion was the Mod. This again was a working class fashion, however the earliest originators of this look were, it seems, kids from secure middle class homes. Most were Jewish and had the money to experiment, presumably they got it from their parents as a lot of them were too young to be at work.

As yet there was no specific look, or any group called Mods. There were a very small number of individuals who were interested in clothes. 'Interested' is to put it mildly because they were completely and utterly clothes obsessed. They were mostly males although there were one or two like-minded girls. They were not a group, just a scattering of daring and determined individual stylists. They were incredibly vain, a bit snobbish and totally narcissistic. At the very beginning of the whole thing they were isolated from, and unaware of, each other. Independently they pursued a common passion.

Ric from Wembley, who later became a Mod, remembers this time. 'I used to knock around with this Jewish guy. We were good friends. He had a couple of other Jewish friends and one of their fathers was in the rag trade. They started getting into clothes very seriously. I was still at school and didn't have any money.

'My friend had left. He didn't have a job though. His Dad had his own business and was doing all right and he used to get money from his parents. He'd just hang around all day or dress up to go up town to get more clothes. He started having his shoes hand-made, and then some of his shirts. There was no way I could keep up with him and his two friends. They all had Italian-style suits, dark blue, and they wore light blue button down collar shirts. He had loads of suits, they were nearly all blue. He wore those sort of Italian-French shoes. Crepe shoes, those crinkly slip-ons, all gathered around the top. I'd never seen shoes like that before. They cost him a fortune. So did his shirts

which were made up to his own designs in Savile Row or somewhere.

'He was amazingly fussy about it all, the three of them were. But they knew exactly what they wanted. They were always talking clothes. It was almost like a religion.'

These teenage Dandies were reacting against the fifties yobbishness. They hated its coarseness and garishness. They identified with what was new and sophisticated. They wanted to be part of all the very modern things that were happening in 1959 and 1960. England at that time was in the middle of the Traditional Jazz (Trad) craze. The charts were full of English versions of Dixieland jazz. Acker Bilk, Kenny Ball, Monty Sunshine and Chris Barber were the big names. However the scruffy cider and beer drinking world of Trad didn't appeal to these individuals. They identified with Modern Jazz and its clean, new, smooth image. They would buy albums by people like the Modern Jazz Quartet, Charlie Mingus, Gerry Mulligan and Dave Brubeck.

It was from their Modern Jazz tastes that they named themselves. They called themselves Modernists.

There were still only a handful but they were noticed and talked about and their clothes copied by others. They would gravitate towards the West End. 'They'd sit around in coffee bars like the Bastille,' said Ric. 'They'd meet up with other guys like themselves and sit and admire each other.'

Slowly their influence spread. Their outlook on things affected other kids who would aspire to be like them. Gradually the Modernists became a minor cult.

The Italian look went through many modifications. Mostly they were just changes of detail and very slight, but a definite direction was emerging.

Most suits were still bought made to measure. So each time one was made it was slightly different to suit each individual. For instance, they had rounded jacket fronts. Two, three or four button jackets. Covered buttons. The box jacket could have small side vents, 1", 2" or 3" long, or a half belt at the back, or both. Cuff could be open, with or without a link button or a butterfly cuff, which is an open cuff coming to a point. Some jackets were very cut-away and rounded to look like a bolero.

Trousers were narrow but varied between 14" to 17" bottoms. There was a brief period of bell bottoms. Then came slanted bottoms, or even stepped bottoms where the trouser leg bottoms were cut at the seams so that the back was lower than the front by about an inch. Trouser legs were also finished with a small slit in the side seam at the bottom, usually anything up to 3" long. There could be little details like small buttons sewn on the seams of trousers just above the shoes. Suits were still predominently blue and dark blue or had strong black and blue stripes. Also another popular fabric then was Prince of Wales check.

The shirts which at first had a short pointed collar

gave way to long pointed collars with a very close gap at the front. This made ties a lot slimmer and the knot smaller. Narrow knitted ties were the favourite.

Shoes were often made to measure, preferably at Stans of Battersea. This was expensive but was the only way the kids could get what they wanted. The extended point shoe, nicknamed the winklepicker, was still in fashion. The points were often 3″ or 4″ long. Sometimes they were made with a cuban heel. Buckles on shoes and side laces came in. Imitation crocodile skin, known as 'mock croc', was a big thing for shoes.

It was also very smart to wear shoes of red or green leather. Casual clothes like cardigans and 'Fred Perrys' started appearing. A 'Fred Perry' was a knitted cotton short-sleeved sports shirt with a three-button opening at the top. It was really designed as tennis wear. Fred Perry, who presumably designed it, had been a famous tennis player. There were cheaper versions but it was better to be seen in the genuine article with the little laurel wreath emblem embroidered on the left breast. It was a very versatile and distinctively Mod item, and could be worn with Levis or a suit. It still looked smart to wear a suit without a tie, *if* you wore a Fred Perry shirt, and this look lasted with one or two modifications (mainly to the suits) throughout the whole Mod era.

Italian hair cuts had come in in about 1960. Not all barbers could do an Italian haircut as most of them still simply cut men's hair rather than styling it, but for about 6/- (as opposed to the normal 2/6d) you could get the 'Perry Como' cut. The style had a different, 'dry' look because kids had no oil or grease on it and in those days it wasn't easy to get out of the barber's without him rubbing some sort of oil into your hair.

After this came the 'College Boy' cut, which was shorter than the 'Perry Como', and then the 'French Crew' which was like a crew cut but longer — about two inches all over. Another new hairstyle was the 'French Crop', which was like a grown out 'College Boy' with a higher parting. All these styles were short, neat and clean-looking — the distinguishing feature of the earliest Mods.

As early as 1959 there were kids with motor scooters and by 1960 there were little gangs known as 'Scooter Boys'. They too were very clothes conscious: one forerunner of the later scooter Mod look. They wore Parkas, ex-army khaki-coloured all-weather cape-shaped coats which they could wear over their outer clothes. They wore them for practical reasons more than for their looks, although later Parkas became fashionable.

Levi jeans caught on about that time. They cost about 42/6d. They were all button fly fronted and stiff as cardboard when you first wore them. Kids had to sit in the bath and shrink them on. They used to scrub them and then later bleach them to get a faded look, the more bleached-looking the better.

The changes in life that were taking place in the late fifties and early sixties were cleverly summed up by Lionel Bart in his song, *'Fings Ain't What They Used To Be'*. Local family grocers were being replaced by Supermarkets. 'Frothy' Coffee Bars and Wimpy bars appeared. 24-hour launderettes took over from laundries, bagwash and municipal wash-houses. It was all part of an Americanisation that was taking place. Modernists identified with all these new 'convenient' innovations. They thought England still too fuddy-duddy and conservative. They were the generation of advertising and soft sell. The advertising industry had been Americanised too since the introduction of commercial television. Modernists really wanted to own that E-type Jag and have that blonde hanging on their arm.

They also looked to the Continent for fashion inspiration. They'd see French students and tourists in the summer who were much better dressed than themselves. So they went to French clubs in London. The most popular were ones catering for French students, *La Poubelle* and *Le Kilt*. Willie Deasey from East London regularly visited these two clubs. 'The clothes the French guys wore were so well-cut. We weren't used to good casual clothes. They had hipster trousers and round-toed shoes, beautiful shoes. They had well-cut suits made from lightweight fabrics. The stuff used to look good for dancing. We used to get all our ideas for clothes from them.'

They immersed themselves in all things French. 'We used to go to see French movies as much as we could,' remembers Johnny Moke, a friend of Willie Deasey's. 'Mostly I couldn't understand a bloody word of it. Next day I'd tell everybody, "Hey, I saw a great French film, you should go and see it, it's absolutely wonderful." I went to see a film called *YoYo*. I sat through about an hour of it and said to my girlfriend, "He's not talking." Afterwards she explained that the star, Marcel Marceau, never talked anyway, he just mimed. I didn't realise, you know, just 'cos it was French I was sitting there.'

Another of Willie and Johnny's friends took it all a bit too seriously. 'We never smoked but would light up a Gauloise just to be seen with it. We all got into the French films and magazines, but Les went berserk. He used to wear a striped jumper and a beret and eat garlic and everything. He started to learn French. We saw him once sitting in Aldgate Wimpy holding up a copy of *Le Soir*. When we went in and joined him we saw that he was really reading the *Sunday Pictorial* which he had concealed in between the middle pages. It was all a pose. There was even a time when we saw him walking around wearing his beret and striped jumper and carrying a loaf of French bread under his arm'.

Of course, Modernists had Continental heroes. There weren't many English stars that they admired, apart from perhaps Sean Connery's James Bond, but they were fans of people like Marcello Mastroianni and Juliette Greco.

Although a Mod look had emerged there was still no sense of common identity that embraced the whole movement. This was probably because Mods existed mostly in clubs and coffee bars and in each others houses. The press hadn't yet 'discovered' them.

They were still very localized. Each area would have its fashion purist as leader and he would influence the kids in his area. They'd see him and his friends in the dance hall or club and copy his clothes, while he in his turn would meet other 'faces' in clubs and coffee bars in the West End and take note of what was being worn by whom. So within the general attitude to clothes and living that had emerged, there were different pockets of kids with different local variations.

Then in 1962, *Town* magazine printed photographs and an interview with some 'faces' from Stamford Hill. One of these was 15-year-old Mark Feld (who later became Mark Bolan and a successful seventies pop star). They talked of their attitude to clothes and bemoaned the difficulty of finding good tailors. 'Bilgorri of Bishopsgate — he's a great tailor . . . . All the faces go to Bilgorri. And John Stephens. He's very good on trousers.' They also spoke of finding cheaper clothes, suits from Burtons and shirts costing 14/6d from C&A. 'Some faces won't look at them because they're only 14/6d. That's just ridiculous,' Mark Feld said, and told of a gingham shirt he'd seen that morning in Woolworths, 'Only ten bob; a few alterations and it would look as good as a four guinea job from John Michael.'

The Town magazine article was the first media coverage of these young devotees of fashion, and it was inspiration and confirmation for all the others. It was in 1962 that all the individual and diverse elements finally fused into the overall Mod style. It was still very male-dominated and largely centred around the London suburbs and the Home Counties, but was gradually spreading out.

It was now important to walk properly, hold a cigarette the correct way and know the right way even to stand. Correct stance was important because a lot of time was spent hanging around posing and talking and showing oneself off. Johnny Moke remembers, 'You'd have to look totally relaxed, but right. You'd have to pose, so you sort of slouched, you put your leg against the wall. To look cool, you'd put your hands in your Levi's or your jacket pocket with your thumbs sticking out.' Rik from Wembley remembers that stance was important. 'Feet had to be right. If you put your hand in your trouser pocket, you never pulled the jacket up so it was wrinkled. You'd have the top button done up and the jacket would be pulled back behind the arm so that you didn't ruin the line. You'd only ever put one hand in your pocket if you were wearing a jacket. It was a bit foppish, but quite subtle.'

There was still difficulty in finding the right kind of clothes. Suits would be made to measure and in London there were shops like John Michael which stocked fairly reasonable stuff, but the real discovery for most kids was His Clothes in Carnaby Street. It's different for anyone who wasn't around then to imagine how revolutionary Carnaby Street was, especially if you see what it has descended to these days.

I first went there with Pete Townshend. Somebody had told us about the street and one day, while we were in the West End we decided to have a look. We couldn't find it at first, it really was a back-street of London. It wasn't a very attractive street either. One side had a huge windowless brick-built warehouse owned by the Electricity Board or someone. There were four, or maybe five, men's clothes shops and a tobacconist's. I can't remember much else and I don't think there was much else. There was more than one shop called His Clothes, then, I think, Paul's and Domino Male and Donis. This day was wet and grey and the street was deserted. But when we saw the clothes we couldn't believe them. It was the more colourful clothes that amazed me: I mean, candy-pink denim hipsters for men? Fantastic. Outrageous.

In most men's outfitters at that time you'd see lines of jackets or trousers or something and they'd all look the same. Some were black, some were dark black, others were jet black and if you wanted to be a little extrovert you could risk a black one with, wait for it, a grey speckle running through it. But in His Clothes not only were there fantastic daring colours, but there were loads of different styles and fabrics. All of this was crammed into a little space with lots of good music coming from speakers on the wall. You could try things on and handle what you liked with out any besuited salesman 'advising' you. The assistants were all very young and friendly and polite. As was John Stephen himself. He called everybody 'Sir' and went to a lot of trouble to be helpful.

There was a sense of excitement in Carnaby Street. It wasn't very well known then but was doing well, and had a growing clientele. I think most of its trade was on Saturdays, since, as I said, it was deserted this particular weekday. The only other person we saw was a tall, well-dressed young negro who bought a pair of the coloured denim hipster trousers. This negro was obviously homosexual and I realised that homosexuals had been buying that stuff for years. They were the only people with the nerve to wear it, but in the early sixties the climate of opinion was changing, the Mods were wearing the more effeminate and colourful clothes of Carnaby Street. John Stephen stated simply that he thought men 'should be able to wear whatever they liked'.

Just around the corner from Carnaby Street was Vince in Newburgh Street, which had been selling flamboyant clothes to homosexuals and showbiz people since 1954. Vince was the forerunner to Carnaby Street. John Stephen worked there as an assistant for a time and then opened up his own business with just £300 capital in Beak Street. The story goes that all his stock was destroyed in a fire and he started up again around the corner in Carnaby Street because the rent was only £10 per week.

Boutiques were only just beginning to happen. In most shops you went in and asked the assistant if you could have the blue shirt in the window, size 14½. The boutiques in Carnaby Street were crammed with clothes and accessories which were hanging up all around the door and everywhere. Shopping was a lot easier and it was fun. His Clothes wasn't expensive either and the clothes were fairly well made for the price, unlike a lot of the rubbish offered later by John Stephen's rivals. It was all very St. Tropez — boutiques, tight hipsters and white flared trousers and matelot shirts. His Clothes used to sell button-down denim shirts in different pale shades of denim. T-shirts appeared for the first time. They were considered very new and 'in' worn with Levis and sneakers. Moccassin shoes appeared and so did reefer jackets which were American sailor jackets in navy blue. Even if you went there regularly each week, there were always new styles in stock.

It later became a 'place to be' when the Mod era was in full bloom. You'd meet people there and hang around talking and getting almost run over. You could bump into Brian Jones, Andrew Oldham, Eric Clapton or 'Rod the Mod', or other aspiring people from the music game buying clothes. Of course, it didn't last all that long before the press went silly about it and you couldn't move for camera crews from Belgian T.V., and tourists. The day Townshend and I first went there we spent a lot of time gazing in with wonder, our noses pressed up against the window. We counted out the money we had, and just about had enough for Pete to buy a pair of socks. I don't think he ever wore them. We returned four days later with some money and bought jackets.

When The Who were later building up their 'supermod' image, Kit Lambert put it about that Pete used to spend £100 a week on clothes. If he did (and he didn't) he wouldn't have found too much in Carnaby Street because it lost its way around 1965 and was full of carnival novelty wear for people up from the provinces who 'swung'.

In 1962 some Mods took up the traditional City Gent look. For a short time a few even copied City gents. Johnny Moke says, 'At one time I used to wear a bowler hat, striped suit and carry an umbrella. Some Mods did that for a while. It didn't last long but it's where the waisted suits came from.'

The waisted suits were taken from the traditional English suit. Instead of the two-seamed box-jacket of the Italian suit, it had an additional centre-back seam. The English suit was more formal-looking and conservative than the casual Continental suit. It was known all over the world. The centre-seam allowed the waisted jackets to have a centre vent as opposed to the side-vents of the Italian jackets. Side-vents were terribly important. They got longer and longer. The 3″ vent became the 4″ and then the 5″. Kids used to buy jackets with side vents and cut them even longer, or get their mothers or sisters to. It got so that they'd have up to 10″ vents in jackets. In the waisted jackets the centre-vents also got longer. It was a matter of being one-up on everyone else: they'd see a jacket with 5″ side vents and go and order one with vents of 6″. One Mod interviewed later about his clothes said that he'd been away from the scene, working abroad, and daren't wear any of his jackets until he found out the length side vents were now.

Backcombing the hair came in. The style was to have a short half-parting high on the head and to backcomb the rest of the hair so it gained height at the back. It was quite difficult to keep this style looking good.

Special 'bobble combs' for backcombing became standard equipment and guys started lacquering hair to keep it in position. Hair could be raised two or three inches with practice, effort and a backcomb. Rod Stewart, who used to be around singing with various Rhythm-and-Blues groups, had the most far-out back-combed hair I ever saw. His hair was longer than most Mods, and it rose up from just in front of his crown to it seemed about 6″ in height and was heavily laquered. Partings were in the middle or sometimes blow waved which raised up the parting. Johnny Moke had this hair style: 'We thought it was very French, it probably wasn't though. I used to go to bed every night in hair rollers, to keep my hair in.' Some Mods would go to a ladies salon, usually after most of the customers had already left, for their hairstyles, although men's barbers had adapted quickly and were now really good at giving these young dudes what they wanted.

As the Mod style gathered momentum it broke away from the suit-oriented look. More casual clothes came in as it got closer to street-level. Cycling shirts and cycling shoes caught on. These were originally bought in the West End at Lonsdale sports shop in Beak Street, but cycling shops were still fairly common then and kids could easily get cycling clothes and shoes. Levis were worn more. A lot of kids could afford this kind of dress whereas they couldn't afford to buy suits. The more purist of the early Modernists didn't approve of widening the style. They thought that it would get diluted and lose its sophistication. They were a bit snobbish but were right in as much as the style did start to get diluted. But the new kids never lost the intensity of the originals, they just broadened it to encompass more.

The early Modernists' interest in Modern Jazz did not happen simply as a reaction against the Trads. It was probably started by black artists with chart hits, like Ray Charles, who released *What'd I say?* in 1959, and Sam Cook, who had hits with *Only Sixteen* and *You Send Me* in the late fifties. The interest in singers like these and in the black Modern Jazz musicians widened to include other black singers and black music. It was difficult to hear much black music on English radio, but there were programmes for American Forces stationed in Europe and kids used to listen to that. Interest in early Blues music grew. Then Soul music and Rhythm-and-Blues were discovered.

Getting hold of any of the records, which were made for the Black market in the States by very small and obscure record companies, was pretty impossible. However, obscure records did eventually appear, through some enlightened importers plus U.S. servicemen and through sailors. That's why Liverpool was so rich in American R&B records.

Kids collected records quite obsessively. Lots of Mods were almost as passionate about acquiring good records as they were about acquiring clothes. Certain record shops that had obscure imports were discovered. The more obscure the better because Mods hated commercialism. They would get hold of, say, *Hey Baby* by Bruce Channel and play it to death, but as soon as it was released and got into the charts they lost interest in it. It was important to hear something first, before anyone else, and to be full of information about obscure recordings by Blues musicians. If someone boasted about some Snooks Eaglin track he'd heard, the thing was to have heard it too and to be able to talk knowledgeably about other Snooks Eaglin material. This process Mods called 'topping up', always being able to be one up on others. It was all done very matter-of-fact but was really taken quite seriously.

It was a bit of a mystery to me how kids built up such good record collections at that time. I was incredibly fortunate, as the two Americans that lived in the flat above the one I shared while at Art school introduced my flat-mate and myself to their record collection, which was amazing. This was about the time they also introduced us to 'certain substances' which were also amazing. They had to leave the country quickly because of the substances and asked us to look after their records. Our humanitarian principles forced us to agree and our compassion resulted in one of the best American record collections around falling into our laps. As my flat-mate was Pete Townshend who played in a group and was to become one of the High Numbers and the driving force of the Who, amongst other things, it isn't difficult to see what a turning point this unexpected windfall was for him. Having thoroughly mastered his Bert Weedon book, he now had a veritable Aladdins cave of albums which included most of the sounds that were the foundations of British rock of the sixties. This collection included all of Jimmy Reed's albums, Chuck Berry, Bo Diddley, Mose Allison, Jimmy Smith, Muddy Waters, John Lee Hooker, Slim Harpo, Lightnin Hopkins, Jimmy Witherspoon, Booker T, Sonny Terry and Brownie McGhee. Little Richard, Jerry Lee Lewis, Carl Perkins, Howling Wolf, Nina Simone, Ray Charles, The Coasters, The Drifters, Jimmy McGriff, Brother Jack McDuff, Big John Patton, Wes Montgomery, Jimmy Giuffre, Chet Atkins, Fats Domino, Mary Wells, James Brown, The Shirelles, Sonny Boy Williamson, The Isley Brothers, The Impressions, The Miracles and a Pat Boone E.P.

Also, art schools were well up musically and in our café opposite the art school the students had half the spaces on the juke box for their own records. Many a *Corona* soft drinks lorry driver would get Jimmy McGriff blasting out when he thought he was getting Miki and Griff. The Mods from the adjoining catering commercial colleges used to get records from the art students.

The early R&B scene was again centred in London. The earliest club was the Ealing Club, which was the first place the Rolling Stones played. The Pretty Things and Alexis Korner played there a lot too. The Stones moved on from the Ealing Club to the Station Hotel in Richmond. They attracted a large following there and moved to the bigger Richmond Athletic ground club house. This was the Crawdaddy Club and the Rolling Stones were the resident group. The Crawdaddy Club became the most important R&B club for Mods outside the West End.

The first R&B club I ever went to was The Railway Hotel in Harrow and Wealdstone. I later ran this club with the High Numbers and the T-Bones as resident groups, but this night I saw the Cyril Davis All-Stars. Cyril Davis and Alexis Korner were the two most important R&B musicians in the country. Until it exploded in late '62, there was only a small following for R&B and the only bands in London were the All Stars and Alexis Korner's Blues Inc. The growing infant R&B scene revolved very much around these two.

The early Stones loose line-up often included Alexis Korner and they played in with Cyril Davis for a time when he had a regular Thursday night at the Marquee club. John Mayall, who later formed John Mayall's Bluesbreakers, from which came half the names that made up the 60's rock establishment, used to play alongside Alexis Korner's band. Others were drawn to these two and passed through and on to form groups of their own.

Cyril Davis, who played the harmonica brilliantly, was probably near 40, balding, and wore lumpy jackets and baggy corduroys. The singer, Long John Baldry, was about 6′ 6″ tall, incredibly thin and young-looking, and wore an immaculate silver grey Mod suit. The All Stars became a big cult thing in London until Cyril Davis's death in early 1964.

The Rolling Stones played early Blues and R&B and Chuck Berry material. They built up a big following including the Mods. But for various reasons the Mods went off the group. I don't know if it was the release of their first record, *Come On*, a not particularly good cover version of a Chuck Berry number, which turned Mods off the group.

The reason was probably that Mods only liked the originals. Like it said in Dobie Gray's *The In Crowd*, '. . . The originals are still the greatest.' The Stones were commercialising coveted Mod favourites like Ben E. King, Chuck Berry and Muddy Waters. Ron Mitchell was a Mod that liked the Stones originally, 'What I couldn't stand was that I'd say to people, "Listen to this" and play some great music that they'd never heard of and they weren't interested. Then the Rolling Stones would do a poxy cover version of it and everybody would say, "Isn't it great? I really like this

R&B, the Stones' kind of sound." I completely went off them when they recorded *You Better Move On*. Arthur Alexander was about three places below God in my estimation and I thought to cover his song was sacrilege. People still think the Stones wrote *It's All Over Now* even today. Mind you we never could stand the Beatles. Some Mods did, but they did all those great Miracles and Marvellettes songs.'

Mods thought the Stones were also a pretty scruffy lot. The Stones gave up their residency at the Crawdaddy club to tour with Bo Diddley in 1963. The Yardbirds took over and were much more acceptable to the Mods. They played more authentic Blues and the guitarist, Eric Clapton, dressed like a Mod. By this time the Beatles had released *Love Me Do* and *Please Please Me* and Merseybeat exploded onto the music scene overshadowing London R&B on the national charts. Mods were not Beatles fans and ignored the top ten. The Merseysound never really caught on in the clubs and dance halls in the South of England.

The term Rhythm-and-Blues covered various kinds of music. Cyril Davis played R&B derived mainly from early country Blues. The Stones and Alexis Korner were more influenced by city Blues. The Beatles and groups like them were mostly impressed by the more commercial R&B of black singing groups such as the Miracles and the Impressions. Musicians like Georgie Fame were also regarded as R&B, and their roots and inspiration came from more jazz-oriented people like Mose Allison, Fats Domino and Ray Charles.

Mods preferred the contemporary U.S. black vocal groups and collected stuff by bands like the Shirelles, Martha and the Vandellas and the Chiffons etc. Tamla was just getting its first successes and this typified the Mods' taste rather than the less smooth, less sophisticated Blues. Mods would collect Jimmy Witherspoon and Muddy Waters to listen to at home, but they wanted to get hold of something they could dance to and John Lee Hooker didn't lend himself too well to the *Block*.

Apart from the Crawdaddy Club, the Mods' mecca was Soho. The Flamingo, which at night called itself the Allnighter, the Scene, and La Discothèque were the main West End Mod Clubs. The resident group at the Flamingo was Georgie Fame and the Blue Flames. The Mods adopted this group. Georgie Fame was very jazz influenced. He had a smooth voice not unlike Mose Allison's and his organ playing was fantastic, like a cross between Booker T and Jimmy Smith. The Blue Flames had a full powerful sound and included two saxophones and conga drums. their repertoire of *Night Train*, *Get on the Right Track Baby*, *Parchment Farm*, *Do the Dog*, *Let the Good Times Roll*, *Green Onions*, *Work Song* and *Shop Around* used to pack out the Flamingo most nights and throughout the weekend. Lots of negro G.I's used to hang around the place and they used to be a source of U.S. records for the Flamingo Mods. The Flamingo was partly responsible for bringing in the West Indian influence. The Bluebeat hats, like bowler hats but with a very short brim and called 'Pork Pie' hats, were first worn by West Indians in the Roaring Twenties club. But the same West Indians frequented the Flamingo and Allnighter as well, and the Mods picked up the style from them. Dances like 'The Dog' and 'The Ska' were also copied from the West Indian dancers at the Flamingo. Mods also liked the Zoot Money Big Roll Band, another jazzy R&B band that played the Flamingo and Allnighter clubs.

Just a few doors down Wardour Street from the Flamingo was La Discothèque. This was probably the first club only to play records and not have live groups. It was exclusively for dancing and had mattresses around the edge of the dance floor for people to rest. Kids used to dance all night up to four o'clock the next morning.

The other main Mod club was the Scene club. It probably was *the* Mod club in Soho and all the important 'faces' would hang out there. Guy Stephens, the D.J. had all the best records long before anybody else. He was in a strong position to do so as he had set up the *Sue* record label and had contacts with practically all the black labels in the States. I used to go along with Townshend to his flat in Regents Park to hear records that the High Numbers might want to play on stage or record. He had hundreds of albums and piles of singles from remote and unknown small record companies. For a fee he'd tape the ones you wanted.

They also had live bands at the Scene. The Animals played there a lot and the High Numbers were resident for a period. They also had black blues bands like Jimmy James and the Vagabonds, Herbie Goins and the Night Timers and black singers like Ronnie Jones.

I mustn't forget the Marquee Club which was originally in Oxford Street in a good-sized and atmospheric basement but moved in 1964 to smaller premises in Wardour Street. Nearly every R&B band played at the Marquee, and it was the main London venue for live bands.

Outside the West End, the music scene in the rest of London and the suburbs was getting frantic. There were lots of new bands both part-time, semi-professional and full time professional outfits, doing the circuit of more and more new clubs.

Another established club, known for Trad Jazz, but changed to R&B was the Eel Pie Island Hotel, situated on Eel Pie Island in the Thames at Twickenham. The Stones, Yardbirds, Cyril Davis and lots of people played Eel Pie Island. The audience used to stand on each others shoulders at some early Stones gigs so that there were two layers of people! The Downliners Sect were resident group for a time in 1964.

The bands that the kids saw in their local club or dance hall were not usually Mod bands. They didn't look like Mods. Sometimes one or two of the band would be Mods but it wasn't usual. The mods liked the bands because they played the sort of music they liked. The kids in the dance halls didn't get any lead in fashion from the groups, as they were usually much smarter and better dressed than the people on stage. The first Mod-looking group were The Who, at the time they became the High Numbers. They were originally called the Detours, and found out there was another group with that name. The name 'The Who' was thought up for them by a friend who was obviously a genius, and one of the reasons I thought it up was that there was this M.C. at the Oldfield Hotel dance-hall in Greenford, where they played regularly, and he loved to have a little joke when introducing the groups. He would say stuff like 'And now I'd like introduce the Detours — the who? Never 'eard of 'em', and other assorted witticisms. I thought we could spike his guns for him. (Townshend incidentally wanted to call the band the Hair. The next day he even suggested a combined name, The Hair and the Who which sounded to me more like a pub than a group).

Anyway, a little later Pete Meaden came along with a plan to turn the group into Mods. Meaden realised that the Mods were not listening to the charts and had no group to focus on. They were missing out on the great English rock thing that was happening since the Beatles had come along and opened the whole thing up. The Who were not Mods: Meaden made them Mods. He got £50 or some ludicrously small figure from their then manager and bought them some Mod clothes. Roger Daltrey was the most Mod looking with his short hair. Meadon bought him a white jacket and black trousers and two-tone shoes. Townshend had an Ivy League jacket with 5″ side vents made for him at Austins in Shaftesbury Avenue. Moon had a cycling shirt and Levis with 1″ turn-ups and white basketball shoes and Entwistle, who called himself Johnny Allison (after his girl friend — not Mose Allison), had Levis and a striped madras jacket. They were all given Mod haircuts and I swear I never laughed even once when Townshend got back that day with his new short hair. Meaden changed the name again from the Who to the High Numbers: 'Numbers' were the little Mods with numbers on their T-shirts.

The Who were a very good band even before Meaden came along. As The Detours they'd put in their apprenticeship playing at least four nights a week at regular venues plus, any other gigs that came along. They had steadily improved and with Townshend's record collection for inspiration they were one of the better semi-professional groups around London. They played numbers by James Brown, Jimmy Reed, Slim Harpo, Mose Allison, Marvin Gaye and Martha and the Vandellas, as well as lots of Chuck Berry and the usual songs most groups in those days did, like *Route 66*, *Fortune Teller*, *Johnny B. Goode* (Entwistle's vocal) *Poison Ivy* and *Road Runner*.

The difference between the Who and most bands was that they were playing more Tamla Motown type R&B. Meaden introduced them to even more Tamla stuff. He used to sound like England's answer to Lord Buckley when he was enthusing about his beloved Smokey Robinson, or so nice Curtis Mayfield. Meaden was so outrageously 100% hip, especially after about eleven o'clock in the morning when he'd had his Drinamyl breakfast. We used to go to De Hems pub and Oyster bar in Soho where Meaden would have contacts in the music business and spend the lunch hour drinking scotch and coke, or wine while he'd try to plug the group. It was whispered that you could buy the bottom three places in a certain top fifty record chart in De Hems Oyster bar. £50 a week for position number 47 and £25 for a week at number 50.

The High Numbers had been playing to Mods as The Who for some time already. They had a strong Mod following at the Goldhawk club in Shepherds Bush, in Forest Hill, at the Trade Union Hall in Watford and at the Railway Hotel, Wealdstone where they had a residency every Tuesday.

At first they rebelled against being dressed up, at least Roger and particularly John did. There were mumblings. John walked through a puddle and the sole of one of his boxing boots came away. They didn't feel like Mods in the clothes Meaden had bought them.

In the hand-out that Meaden issued with the release of *I'm The Face*, the group's first record he says, 'The important thing about the High Numbers which is immediately noted on meeting them is that nothing is contrived or prefabricated about them and this can be said particularly in the field of clothes . . .' Actually the important thing which was immediately noted, after their first attempt was, I think, that they *were* contrived and prefabricated *especially* in the field of clothes. A Mod wasn't simply somebody wearing the right clothes. Perhaps some were but this was the West End. It was Pete Meaden himself who used to keep rabitting on about 'living on the pulse of the city' and 'becoming neat, sharp and cool, an all-white Soho negro of the night.' He was very poetic because he actually *believed* in the Mod lifestyle and was very eloquent about his ideal.

The High Numbers soon got things sorted out. John bought some better-fitting and more stylish jackets, some out of his own money, and they all had some clothes made to measure. By the time the record and hand-out appeared they looked much better. They were never going to be as chic as the top faces, but they looked quite sharp. They were accepted by the ultra-critical Mods (though not by all of them), primarily because of their playing which was 'electric', and not because they were fashion leaders.

The record got nowhere. It wasn't distributed properly. But it got them noticed and they became part of the Soho scene. They now had a residency at the Scene club. *Fabulous* magazine said, 'You see they're up-to-dates with a difference. They're even ahead of themselves.'

The group were bought from Meaden by Chris

Stamp and Kit Lambert for a few hundred quid. They carried on with the direction begun by Pete Meaden but with the capital to finance their plans.

Lambert and Stamp changed the name back to the Who. The group made it because they were about the most exciting thing in the clubs and because Townshend began writing his own material which was raw and edgy and brilliant. The early Who singles, although coming at the end of Mod, all perfectly illustrate the period. Pete Meaden said soon after that he turned up to a gig at the Aquarium ballroom in Brighton one weekend to see the Who, and couldn't get in because it was too packed with his beloved Mods.

Mods were more interested in themselves and each other than in girls. The girls were fairly unattractive and independent. It was a relief for them not to have to be feminine or painted up, and to be able to assume a more relaxed role sexually. Although one female Mod from the time, Sara Brown from Kensington, remembers some of the frustration girls felt: 'The guys were so preoccupied with their clothes. It got to be a big deal to have a conversation with a guy and we thought we were very lucky if one of these gorgeous creatures actually *danced* with us.' The boys *were* effeminate and used to fuss about and preen in front of the mirror, but they weren't homosexual. There might have been a homosexual element, but then there might also have been among Rockers, and it wasn't particularly important. There was a time when Mod boys used eye make-up and mascara.

Bill Norman explains their motives: 'When you were at work, you were a nobody. So when you put on your suede or mohair suit and Desert Boots and go to the dance hall, you want to be a somebody to your mates. It's your mates you want to impress, not particularly the girls. You make a statement through your clothes, or your dancing, or your scooter.'

The amphetamines that Mods swallowed took away their sex drive. That could be the main reason why they seemed completely to ignore the girls. It could also be that the smart Mod was like a peacock strutting about in front of the peahens. He used his apparent lack of interest to attract the girls.

'You had to be cool. To be chasing birds was seen as soft, a bit sentimental. You didn't want to lose face with the other guys,' points out Bill Norman. Willie Deasey remembers 'One reason why you didn't want to take a girl out was that you couldn't afford to. In those days the bloke was supposed to pay for the girl. Blokes would spend all their money on clothes. Girls were expensive. If you did take a girl to a dance, you'd say "I'll see you in there at 8-30." That way you didn't have to pay her bus fare and entrance money. I had no money for anything but clothes and dancing. I mean you could always pick girls up at parties and stuff.'

Mod had now grown and stretched itself all over England. The small elite of esoteric fashion fanatics with their attention to style and detail gave the less intense Mods something to aspire to. Jack English from Leicester used to come down to London every Friday and spend the weekend either in the clubs or searching out clothes. He recalls, 'There probably were only about twenty *real* true Mods in the whole country.' At any rate, few actually stayed true to the Modernist ideal throughout the whole of the first half of the sixties with the genuine Mod's dedication. It didn't just take a lot of money to keep ahead for so long a period — some of the original Modernists had now got married and focussed their energy on other things. (Marriage was known, sometimes kids would visit a holiday camp and forget their purple hearts.)

More and more of the younger, newer kids went around in groups. A mod would have at least one suit in mohair. Two-tone mohair was popular. It was one colour when viewed from one angle and a different colour seen from another. Usually red and green two-tone, mustardy gold, dark blue, grey, green and ice-blue were the popular colours. Still with the narrow lapels but with either side vents, or a centre vent. The suits would be pressed before wearing. Kids would often take the suits to dances in bowling bags or on hangers in a polythene bag and change into them when they got there. I heard of some kids going to a dance hall on a bus and getting thrown off the bus because they wouldn't sit down even though there were empty seats. They didn't want to crease their trousers.

White suits were very flash. White linen jackets caught on and if you couldn't afford the real thing you could wear an 'ice cream' jacket, the ones that had the kind of buttons found on overalls.

The Harrington jacket had come in. That's the casual zip-up jacket, usually in suede, inspired by Rodney Harrington, a character in the American T.V. soap opera *Peyton Place*.

Raoul shoe shop in Carnaby Street was the best place for shoes unless you were having them hand-made. Round-toed and almond-toed shoes had been in. Chisel-toed shoes, winklepickers with the point chopped off appeared and disappeared briefly. Hush Puppies were favourites as they were considered good to dance in. The most distinctively Mod shoes were Clarks desert boots. Running sneakers looked good with Levis and Fred Perrys' or T-shirts. T-shirts with initials sewn on were made up by the kids themselves, based on the U.S. campus T-shirts. Later, a clothing company started selling T-shirts with a big Y on the front from Yale University, and that look was adopted by the younger 'Moddy boys'.

Johnny Moke gives an insight as to how a fashion craze could begin. 'We went to a bowling alley wearing some old plimsoles. We hired a brand new pair of bowling shoes and afterwards I walked out with mine. That weekend we went to Clacton. It was the weekend of the first trouble. I'd taken off the big number 8 that was stuck on the back and was the only guy walking around Clacton with bowling shoes on. When I went to Brighton about six weeks later, half the kids had bowling shoes.'

Although girls appeared to be dragging along behind the boys everywhere, their fashions were as important to the Mod look as the guys. In the fifties, girls were still corsetted and strapped-up in suspender belts, pantie-girdles and all that 'corrective' brassière stuff. Girls were wearing what older women were wearing. It was a very formal style of dress. The fifties teenage fashions that emerged for girls were American and came from teenage films — college campus stuff, bobby sox, peddle pusher pants, hoop skirts and pony tails.

The early Modernist girls each worked on their own styles. There were less of them even than the few boys. Again they all had a similar attitude to clothes, although once again they were still just a collection of like-minded people and not yet united in a style. One definite look for early girl Modernists was of flared barathea skirts and 'man-style' shirts. This was a relief from the look of the fifties, and the beginnings of a new style for girls generally. Modernist wanted to look self-assured, smart and worldly. They introduced their own style of make-up that was very new and modern. It got away from the Doris-Day-and-freckles look. It was more Juliette Greco and smokey French nightclubs.

Make-up was very important. Like clothes, the face had to be immaculate but, not in a traditional feminine way — more like a drawing. Lipstick disappeared, and for the first time since the twenties the eyes became the most prominent feature. The look at first had no eye-shadow, just a thin black line. This look continued throughout the period, developing and becoming more exaggerated with heavy false eyelashes and painted lower lashes eventually turning into the heavily-blacked eyes and no eyebrows of the later Mods. The girls would pluck out the hairs of their eyebrows and sometimes paint in a very thin line where they had been, or else leave them bare. They would use a black powder from India called Kohl to apply to their eyes for a sort of sooty-rimmed look. I remember some girls with very obvious white highlighting, and later using white lipstick.

The bouffant hair style was replaced by flat straight hair. It had to be as straight as possible and girls went to all sorts of trouble to get it and keep it straight. The styles were very classic. Parted in the centre, chin length, or the same style but with a deep fringe sometimes almost into the eyes. It was a very simple hair style but had to be just perfect. Girls would spend hours getting it straight and then laquered into position.

As the shops didn't sell the kind of things they wanted, Modernist girls used to make their own clothes. They used very traditional fabrics at first like pinstripes and flannels. Girls started wearing men's trousers. In those days, the trousers that were designed for women had the opening at the side and were cut differently to men's. They had wider hips and narrower waists but looked awful, so girls bought trousers designed for men, narrow hips, front openings and all. There were no deliberately designed unisex clothes then.

Marks and Spencer's twin-sets, usually in maroon, navy or grey, were worn with A-line skirts. Girls or their mothers would make up shift-dresses which had cut-away armholes. These shift-dresses were seen a lot as they were ideal to dance in. The early girl Mods wore no jewellery apart from things like cufflinks for their button-down mens shirts. Later on they wore canvas striped watch-straps. The 'Cleopatra' hair style came in: very dark and immaculate looking, like Liz Taylor's hair when she played Cleopatra in the film.

In 1960 pointed-toed shoes were 'out', but the shoes still had narrow toes. It took another year or so for round toes to come in. The chisel toe came and went briefly, then the almond toe, the front getting more and more rounded off until it turned eventually into granny shape. Girls would rummage around old ladies' shoe departments for the right sort of 'clumpy' shoe. The Granny shoes, which Mod girls would get from shops like K Shoes, were round-toed shoes with a strap which fastened to a little boot button on the side. The heel was about 1½" high and very wide and solid looking. They were very cheap, only 19/6d or something. They were nearly always black or brown but a similar shoe made for tap dancing with a 2" wooden stack-heel was available in scarlet and occasionally other colours from Anello and Davide, the dance shoe specialists in Covent Garden. These were worn without the 'taps' on.

A good selection of Granny shoes were available from old-established ladies' shoe emporiums like Babers in Regent Street. They must have wondered what happened to them when they were being invaded by these black-eyed pale-skinned strange young creatures eager to buy masses of their 'sensible' shoes.

Another Mod look for girls was the 'Hush Puppies and Ski pants' look. These girls had short hair like a boy's, and wore nylon macs. The macs weren't see-through macs, they were from Italy and were either navy blue, brown or bottle-green. Mod girls used to walk around in pairs, arm-in-arm, swinging their B.E.A. shoulder-bags, as they did their clothes-buying in Carnaby Street's male boutiques.

They also wore long straight skirts to 3" below the knee with a fan pleat at the centre back, in herringbone, or navy, or grey pinstripe. They also wore straight-leg hipster trousers, usually in white, and madras jackets. It was quite revolutionary in those days for girls to wear trousers. Cathy McGowan hit the headlines when she was refused entry into the Savoy because she was wearing trousers.

As the boys got more feminine, so the girls got more masculine. They wore flat shoes, short hair and shapeless skirts and sweaters with no feminine curves showing. They seemed to be trying to look more and more butch. The boys had a style and an independence that the girls had to adapt to. 'The guys weren't going out to "pull" the girls, so the girls became part of the gang and were accepted as "one of the boys". So they

continued on page 122

FOR THE MODS

by
JULIAN MAURICE
of Chesham, Bucks

MODERNISTS, or Mods for short, account for about 35 per cent of Britain's male teenage population. Their fashions are the furthest-out, the most up-to-the-second of any, and the male Mod probably devotes between a quarter and a third of his weekly income to his appearance.

As such, they represent a valuable clientele to the men's hairdresser who is prepared to give them the sleek, carefully-groomed styles they are looking for.

All Mod styles have a common factor: they are round (high on top) and low (neckline an inch or so from the collar).

Most important, to maintain the

● Continued on page 5

Before styling (left), the model had long hair swept forward in a Beatle fringe. Below, the stylist combs the hair into an outline of the finished style, whilst soaking it in razor-cutting lotion prior to shortening

Bulk is reduced by careful razor-cutting all over. Here again the stylist is bearing in mind the shape aimed at, cutting with backward movements from the forehead, and following the natural line

Mod Cut
—continued

Mod look, the wearers will become regular visitors to your salon.

The Nashville, based on the sculptured Mod cut, was dressed for HAIRDRESSERS' JOURNAL by 19-year-old Julian Maurice, who was placed second to Joe Gleeson of the British competitors in the Men's European championships in Stuttgart.

It is named after the town which is home of America's music industry, and which first brought to the world 'rhythm'n'Blues—a style of beat music currently very popular with Britain's teenagers.

The hairdresser will lose many Mod clients if the finished style is too short on top. In this case the model had extremely long thick hair, about six inches all over, dressed forward in a Beatle-style fringe.

Obviously this length had to be removed, but care was taken that appearance of length was not destroyed by shortening. Final length on the crown was between three and four inches.

Hair dressed in a Mod style should never be less than two-and-a-half

Above: When razor-tapering the back of the head, movement should be out towards the sides to avoid any ridges

Below: With tapering completed, the hair at the temples follows the natural lines of the finished style

Above: To ensure an even hairline at the front, the temples are tapered with a downward movement on to the model's face

Below: Check to ensure that all ends are correctly tapered. There is no abrupt change in the thickness throughout the length

inches on the crown. If it is, it should be razor-polished rather than tapered, simply thinned and tidied to allow for growth.

The head was thoroughly shampooed to remove all grease, and then brushed through with a tapering brush to ascertain the natural lay of the hair.

Lotion

Next the stylist doused the hair in razor-cutting lotion, combing the hair into a rough semblance of the finished style with a front-to-back movement.

Where the hair is extremely bulky, this is reduced by careful razoring all over, again following a rough outline of the finished style.

Once bulk and length are reduced to reasonable proportions, the hair can be razor-tapered, starting at the back of the head from a point about an inch below the crown.

The razor is moved outwards from a line drawn from this point towards

● Continued on page 7

Sculptured 'Mod' Style

● Continued from page 5

the sides, rather than straight down. This prevents any "steps" at the back, which can ruin an otherwise good style.

When using this technique, the overall length is only reduced where necessary to tidiness, and the stylist aims for a flat appearance at the back of the head. The hair is left as low as is practicable.

When tapering, the razor is applied lightly to each mesh of hair, using a gentle stroking movement.

Then, starting at a point about two inches above each ear, the sides were tapered downwards to the hairline.

The front was similarly tapered, using the same technique in a series of backward movements from the forehead.

The temples and fringe were razored

downwards, following the natural hair line to ensure an even length all round. When treating the fringe, it is important not to start too high, or it will tend to stand away from the forehead in the finished style.

The evenness of the tapering over the whole head was then checked, and the ear and neckline cleaned with scissors and razor.

Crown lift

Finally, the hair was brushed down to the roots, and the brush twisted up and forwards while the hair is dried over it, giving lift at the crown.

It is this which distinguishes the round look of the Mod style from the squarer shapes of past fashions.

The finishing touches were added with a halo net and a small amount of lacquer. On no account should a greasy dressing be used.

When tapering the fringe, hair should be combed forward on to the forehead (above). Below, hair is dried and lifted over a brush

Drying is then completed using a halo net. Note in the picture below the low neck and modern rounded lines of the finished style

Final touches are added with the styling brush flat against the head. The hair should now hold with the minimum of lacquer (below)

rry

TOP

HEAD

. . .

heroes!
s of the
world
ng the
of the

cutter"
k from
s com-

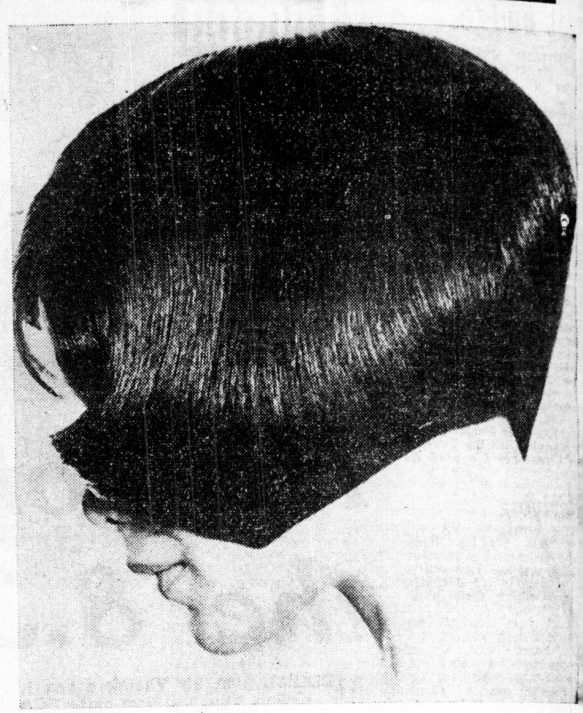

The famous
short blunt
cut of Vidal
Sasscon that
has cut a
great swathe
among Mod
girls, round
the world.
First cut on
the long, dark
tresses of
film star
Nancy Kwan, this is the look that took New York
by storm. Lucky New Yorkers will soon be able to get
the Real McCoy cut at his New York "branch." Prices
here are from 1 gn. for shampoo and set, 25s. for a cut.

DESERT BOOT
*Plantation
Crepe Rubber Soles*

27

DAILY MAIL, Tuesday, September 15, 19

It's a r

NEWSIGHT

The people who buy

Shop assistant COLIN ASHTON, 18, of Stamford Hill, London, earns £12 weekly, lives with his grandmother. Gives her £3 weekly, spends £9 on clothes. A year ago he left London to work in the pro... since; has just returned to find his Mod clothes out of date. ("I can't go out in a pointless jacket, people would look.")

Scooter salesman LEN... 18, from Roehampton, earns £10 weekly, spe... on clothes. Gives £2... sister-in-law for housel... Owns 20 woolly shi... pairs of trousers, is sa... a 26gn. suit. ("I've g... suits, but the style's... Favours: Emerald green... jacket (18gns.) with... green leather collar and... flaps.

Shop manager KEITH LEWIS, 18 of Highgate, London, owns nine suits, 30 pairs of trousers (20 hipsters), 18 shirts ("I've been clearing out so I'm rather low"), 30 different handkerchiefs, six polo-necked sweaters, 40 ties. Used to go without food to buy clothes. Would spend most of his salary on clothes, but is "saving up to marry."

Typist JANE O... 36-22-36 (18), of Ha... London, earns £8... spends £5 on clothes, ...ably men's (slacks, and jumpers). Owns... of men's trousers... hipster slacks are tig... better styled"), 20... jumpers, seven T-shirts,... much of her free... Carnaby-street watching... changes.

Apprentice tailor TONY MIDDLETON, 18, of Hampstead, London, earns £9 weekly, spends £3 on clothes. Owns 15 shirts, seven sweaters, six pairs of trousers, six pairs of shoes (all with Cuban heels). Spends £1 every week, another £1 going on H.P. payments towards his £92 guitar ("I'll pay it off over two years"). Lives in a flat with a friend. His father, a W.O.2 in the Green Howards, is in Germany.

Advertising assistant G... LONGLEY, 19, of Bexle... Kent, earns £10 weekl... parents £2, spends... clothes. He has 15... seven pairs of trouser... pair of shoes. ("The... all right for casual cloth... you can do better for...ing.")

→17   →17A   →18   →18A

od, mod, mod, mod world

he sales start today in Carnaby-street, where the moddest Mods buy the gearest Gear. Here are 200 yards f hipster trousers, suede jackets, tab-collar shirts and bikini underpants in red, white and blue. As e nine men's boutiques, tucked away behind Regent-street, unload dated stock, a Kilburn factory is ready stockpiling next summer's styles. This is part of the lightning-change world of the Mods...

The things they buy

Advertising executive STEPHEN CHASEY, 21, of Berkeley-square, London, earns £13 weekly, gives £2 to his parents, spends £2 10s. a week on clothes. Owns eight pairs of trousers, 12 shirts, four jackets, three suits. Believes the Carnaby-street shops were at their best two years ago (" The styles all seem a bit crude now "). Visits Carnaby-street two days a week keeping an eye on fashions.

Trainee draughtsman MARTIN SINGLETON, 18, of Watford, Hertfordshire, lives at home. Earns £7 weekly, spends £1 10s. on clothes. Owns 25 shirts, three pairs of slacks, five jerseys (" I think that the gear-mad-Mods are stupid to spend almost all their money on clothes. I'm running a scooter and can't afford more ").

Art student FABIO NICOLI, 17, of Norwich, second-year student (graphic design) at Norwich Art School, earned £90 during the summer, working as a restaurant cook in Great Yarmouth. Spent three-quarters of it in Carnaby-street " Mod " shops. Owns ten shirts, all woollen (no ties needed), five pairs of shoes, three pairs of trousers.

Britain's teenagers will spend £220 million this year on clothes. Today's Top Mod buys :

Suits :	From 20gn. for a ready-made, to 60gn. a silk tailor-made. IN : Mohair and " tonic " (heavy weave mohair) ; slim lapels, 8" jacket vents, hipster trousers with 15" bottoms (no turn-ups), silk-lined in red, green, blue.
Shoes :	From 63s. Italian " Zigonis " (one of 30 designs) to hand-made Italian crocodile-skin 17gn. IN : Moccasin slip-ons and light chukka boots.
Trousers : and belts :	From 49s. 6d. to 7gn. IN : Cordu-roy hipsters, riding on the hips with 15" bottoms ; belts, from 25s. IN : Matching watch-strap 10s.
Shirts :	From 49s. 6d. to 84s. IN : Pastel colours, long pointed button-down collars.
Ties :	From 12s. 6d. to 45s. IN : 2in.-wide knitted wool ; also black-leather, suede, Madras cotton.
Waistcoats :	From 30s. to 7gn. IN : Black, red, blue leather. Worn without jacket to show off shirt.
Jackets :	From 6gn. to 25gn. IN : Suede and denim ; centre vents 8-10in., reaching small of back.
Underwear :	10s. 6d. Mini-briefs. IN : String vests, worn also as T-shirts.
Cufflinks :	From 12s. 6d. to 25s. a pair. IN : Ceramic, old coins.
Cardigans :	From £3 10s. to 7gn. IN : Plain colours, no decoration.

The man who SELLS

JOHN STEPHEN, Fashion High Priest, outside one of his Carnaby-street shops . . .

TEN years ago John Stephen, 28, Glasgow-born, was working in a sheet-metal factory. Today he is the High Priest of Male Teenage Fashion.

He owns 18 Mod clothes shops : six in Carnaby-street, ten scattered across London, two in Brighton. He is nego-tiating for another three shops and a store.

He denies being a million-aire ; is not far off it. He employs no designers (" The fashion ideas come out of my head "), has no office (" My managers have ; I use theirs ").

Stephen's shops have names like Male West One, Mod Male, His Clothes.

His shops are often managed by teenagers wearing Mod clothes to advertise new styles.

Stephen arrived in London nine years ago from Scotland, £14 in his pocket. (" Father wanted me to be a draughts-man, I chose fashion ").

He worked in Moss Bros. for nine months as a sales-man, went to a men's wear shop, opened his first (rent : £10 a week) shop in Carnaby-street, 1958.

Today the week'y rent of shops in the street is £120.

He gives two reasons for his success :

1. His own hard work (" Don't finish until 9 or 10 ; then there's only time for a meal and bed ")

2. The fact that no one was catering for the Mod market until he arrived.

Stephen, unmarried, has a maisonette in King's-road, Chelsea, runs a Rolls-Royce (cost : £7,000), Hillman Minx convertible (£1,000), has an 11-month-old white Alsatian, Prince.

He gets ideas for teenagers'

SQUEEZED between the Mod boutiques is Inderwick's (est. 1797), oldest pipe makers in the country. Sales of gimmick pipes (cost : 1s. to 21s.) and Continental tobaccos have doubled since the Mod invasion. Mods buy them as part of their sharp gear.

fashions by watching cus-tomers in his shops. He noticed them fluffing up their collars as they tried on suits, realised that subconsciously, teenagers wanted collars to be deeper.

He introduced them 18 months ago. The style swept the country. He introduced the fly-fronted shirt (it hides the buttons under a fold). The idea came from dress shirts. It worked.

Often Stephen works from " the local caff," does business deals on the Carnaby-street pavements. He has 60 p.c. of the shares in his company. Co-director Bill Franks, 26, has the remaining 40 p.c.

Stephen has 12 suits (" I don't need any more "), bought out a Kilburn clothes factory, Lewis Brothers (est. 1935), a year ago.

He has 120 employees, makes a point of designing leisure clothes for pop groups, film stars. His shops are decorated with glossy show-business pictures. Teenagers copy their ideas.

His only relaxation : week-end horse-riding at Lewes, Sussex.

IF YOU CAN'T BEAT 'EM—JOIN 'EM

A classic Mod style by BARRY WARD
of John Anthony's salon at Twickenham

JOHN ANTHONY, who took over his salon at Heath Road, Twickenham, last September, has a number of salons catering for both men and women.

He says that in West London, an enormous number of the young men who come into his salons want Mod styles.

"This is where we've got to join them —not fight them," says John Anthony. "These boys will go to the hairdresser *when they know that the hairdresser can do what they want.*"

He told the story of a 14 year old boy who, finally cajoled by his mother into visiting the salon, had his hair cut exactly the way *he* wanted it—and returned two weeks later with some friends.

"He didn't believe that when he went to the hairdresser he would get the style he really wanted. Rather than have anything else, he would have stayed away. When he found that he *could* get what he really wanted, he became a firm and regular client."

To win your untapped Mod clientele, study the classic Mod cut featured here by one of John Anthony's stylists, Barry Ward. He, himself, wears his hair in a similar style.

Mr. Anthony remarked that when Mods coming to the salon for the first time saw Barry's hair, they knew that here was a salon where they would get the styles they wanted.

● *More details on page 8*

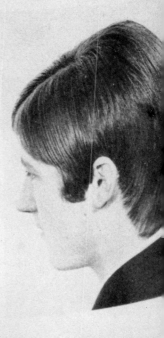

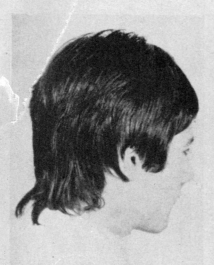

The result of eight to nine weeks' growth—long, straggly hair at the nape

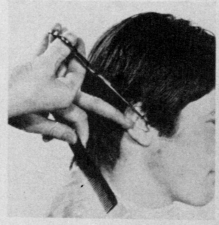

Side hair forward of the ears is very full in this style, but is not untidy. Careful trimming with scissors achieves correct effect. John Anthony allows little use of electric cutters for lining-out on neck lines and round ears in his salons. He prefers the more natural line produced by scissors

No compromise— it's razor cutting only!

JOHN ANTHONY'S attitude to styling is uncompromising. All bulk reducing is done with a razor. No thinning scissors are used by any of his stylists.

Most lining-out of napes and round the ears is done with scissors. On the rare occasion when a clipper is used it always has a 0000 head.

Fine stream

Wide dryer nozzles are thinned out with pliers to achieve an even finer stream of air than normal. "We burn out of lot of elements," says Mr. Anthony, "but the improvement in results is worth it."

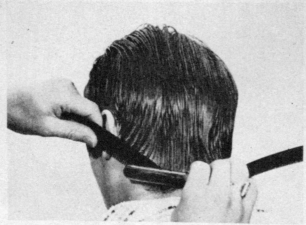

After shampooing, hair at the nape is razor-cut right down to the ends. Nape line is cut with the scissors after shampoo, but before razoring. There is little nape tapering. Hair is lifted on the crown and blended in, but not down to the nape

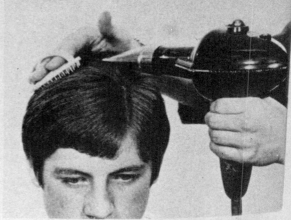

A round, plastics massage-brush is used in pre-drying, before blow-styling begins. This enables control of the general direction of the hair to be maintained, while allowing free passage of warm air to speed the drying

During drying, hair is lifted with hog-bristle styling brush. Lift may drop out at first styling, but is retained naturally after several sessions. It can be further induced by fluffing up the hair with a comb but not back-combing

Final blow-styling is effected with the hog-bristle, flat section brush, but not a net

How to Cut the New French Line

THIS is a classic interpretation of the new Club line for men, launched by the French men's hairdressing *Syndicat*. It is quiet and sober in its design but smart and groomed enough for any age group.

The hair is a little longer than in most recent men's lines. It is not so much thinned by the razor as carefully refined.

Fig. 1.—After having put in the parting (1) make a division through the hair just above the temple (A).

By making a second division a little lower (B), one can shield the "shoulder" meshes which corre-'spond to the area of the greatest volume in the finished style.

The base of the sides is thinned vertically according to the shape of the head.

Fig. 2.—The back and nape hair is reduced with the razor, the scissors being used to control only the extreme points.

All the overlapping meshes on the top of the head must be gone over again very lightly with the razor to obtain a good blending of the points, while retaining fullness just below the parting.

Fig. 3.—In dressing out, secure volume at the sides by taking a small round styling brush and, having determined the thickness of the mesh (1) place the brush at the root (2). Lift the hair with a turning movement while directing the hot air jet from the dryer on to top of the hair (3).

Fig. 4.—To obtain a natural volume at the level of the parting, force the roots a little with the comb *against* the natural direction of the hair growth.

Except for smoothing the hair, take care not to flatten the volume which has been achieved.

by

Fernand Gautier

Member of the Syndicat de la Haute Coiffure Masculine and of the Comité Artistique de la Coiffure Francaise

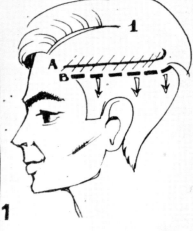

1

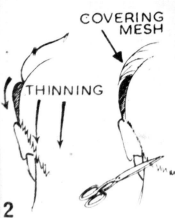

COVERING MESH

THINNING

2

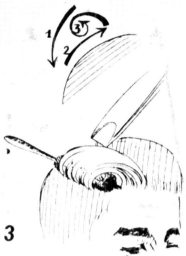

3

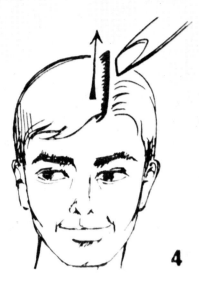

4

34

ATLANTIC
45 RPM
AT 4003
JAMAICA SKA
THE SKA KINGS

BLUE BEAT
A "Buster" Recording
Copyright Control
Recording first published 1963
45/BB 170
(45/SB 3379)
MADNESS
(Prince Buster)
PRINCE BUSTER
MELODISC RECORDS LTD.

PYE INTERNATIONAL
45 RPM
1.45.1238-A
JEWEL MUSIC
7N.25238
RECORDING FIRST PUBLISHED 1964
HI-HEEL SNEAKERS
(R. Higgenbotham)
TOMMY TUCKER
A Checker, U.S.A., Recording

LONDON
AMERICAN RECORDINGS
MADE IN ENGLAND
45 R.P.M.
45-HL 9523
YOU BETTER MOVE ON
ARTHUR ALEXANDER

fontana
45 MONO
TF 520
270130 TF
A
GETTING MIGHTY CROWDED
(Van McCoy)
BETTY EVERETT
A Vee-Jay recording

TOP RANK
INTERNATIONAL
MADE BY ELECTRIC AND MUSICAL INDUSTRIES LTD. IN GT. BRITAIN
45 R.P.M.
JAR-520
Lorna Music
("Herald" Recording)
STAY
(M. Williams)
MAURICE WILLIAMS & The Zodiacs

COLUMBIA
45 R.P.M.
IVAN MOGULL MUSIC LTD
DB 7205
SOLD IN U.K. SUBJECT TO RESALE PRICE CONDITIONS. SEE PRICE LISTS
An Okeh Recording
UM, UM, UM, UM, UM, UM
(C. Mayfield)
MAJOR LANCE
Arranged J. Pate
Producer Carl Davis
MADE IN Gt. BRITAIN

Red Bird
MADE IN ENGLAND
45 RPM
HILL & RANGE (LON.)
RB10 024
RB10 024-A
MB
IKO IKO
(R. & E. Hawkins, J. Johnson)
THE DIXIE CUPS

Stateside
MADE IN GT. BRITAIN
45 RPM
Hunter Music Ltd.
45KR-4382
An Amy Recording
SOLD IN U.K. SUBJECT TO RESALE PRICE CONDITIONS. SEE PRICE LISTS
SS 342
Recording first published 1964
KING OF KINGS
JIMMY CLIFF
E.M.I. RECORDS LIMITED

MOCKINGBIRD
(G. Foxx, I. Foxx)
Saturn Music
Sue RECORDS
WI-301
INEZ FOXX
(Vocal accompaniment C. Foxx)

LONDON
AMERICAN RECORDINGS
MADE IN ENGLAND
45 R.P.M.
Recorded by TAMLA, Detroit
45-HL 9276
E/T
SHOP AROUND
(Gordy, Robinson)
THE MIRACLES

Stateside
MADE IN GT. BRITAIN
45 RPM
Aberbach (London) Ltd
45KR-4157
A Tamla-Motown Recording
SS 228
HEAT WAVE
(Holland—Dozier—Holland)
MARTHA & THE VANDELLAS
Producers Holland—Dozier
E.M.I. RECORDS LIMITED

LONDON Dot RECORDS
AMERICAN
45 r.p.m.
HLD 9751
WIPE OUT
THE SURFARIS

ATLANTIC
45 RPM
Belinda Music
BIEM/NCB
AT.4006
MERCY, MERCY
(Covay, Ott)
DON COVAY AND THE GOODTIMERS

PYE INTERNATIONAL
45 RPM
COPYRIGHT CONTROL
1.45.1231-A
7N.25231
RECORDING FIRST PUBLISHED 1963
LOUIE LOUIE
(Richard Berry)
THE KINGSMEN
A Wand, U.S.A., Recording

ATLANTIC
45 RPM
S
AT.4011
WHAT'CHA GONNA DO ABOUT IT
DORIS TROY

M.G. BLUES
Saturn Music
Sue RECORDS
WI-303
JIMMY McGRIFF

Blue Beat
Melodisc Records Ltd
45 R.P.M.
M.C.P.S.
B.2
V.I.B
Made in England
All Rights of the Manufacturers and of the owner of the Recorded work Reserved
Unauthorised Public Performance, Broadcasting and copying of this Record Prohibited
("Main" Recording)
DUMPLINS
(Ragby)
BYRON LEE
THE DRAGONNAIRS

Stateside
MADE IN GT. BRITAIN
45 RPM
Florentine Music
RECORDING FIRST PUBLISHED 1961
(45-KR-3069)
("Main" Recording)
45SS-135
HIDE AND GO SEEK—PART I
(Bunker Hill)
BUNKER HILL
E.M.I. RECORDS LIMITED

LONDON
AMERICAN RECORDINGS
MADE IN ENGLAND
45 R.P.M.
Recorded by PHILLES, Hollywood
NCB
57 Savile Row
HLU 9773
THEN HE KISSED ME
(Spector, Greenwich, Barry)
THE CRYSTALS

ATLANTIC
45 RPM
Belinda Music
584001
Under licence from Atlantic Recording Corp., U.S.A.
WHEN A MAN LOVES A WOMAN
(Lewis/Wright)
PERCY SLEDGE
Produced by Martin Greene & Quin Ivy
FULTON RECORDS LIMITED

LONDON
AMERICAN RECORDINGS
MADE IN ENGLAND
45 R.P.M.
HL-U 9943
Recorded by PHILLES, Hollywood
N.C.B.
B.I.E.M.
C. Bens
Screen Gems
Columbia M.
YOU'VE LOST THAT LOVIN' FEELIN'
(Spector, Mann, Weil)
THE RIGHTEOUS BROTHERS

Brunswick
45
MADE IN ENGLAND, BRUNSWICK LTD., LONDON
ORIGINAL RECORDING AND LICENSED BY DECCA RECORDS INC NEW YORK U.S.A.
Leeds Music Ltd.
M.C.P.S.
05942
S
1—2—3
(Madara, White, Borisoff)
LEN BARRY

HITCH HIKE PT. I
Copyright Control
Sue RECORDS
WI-305
RUSSELL BYRD

45

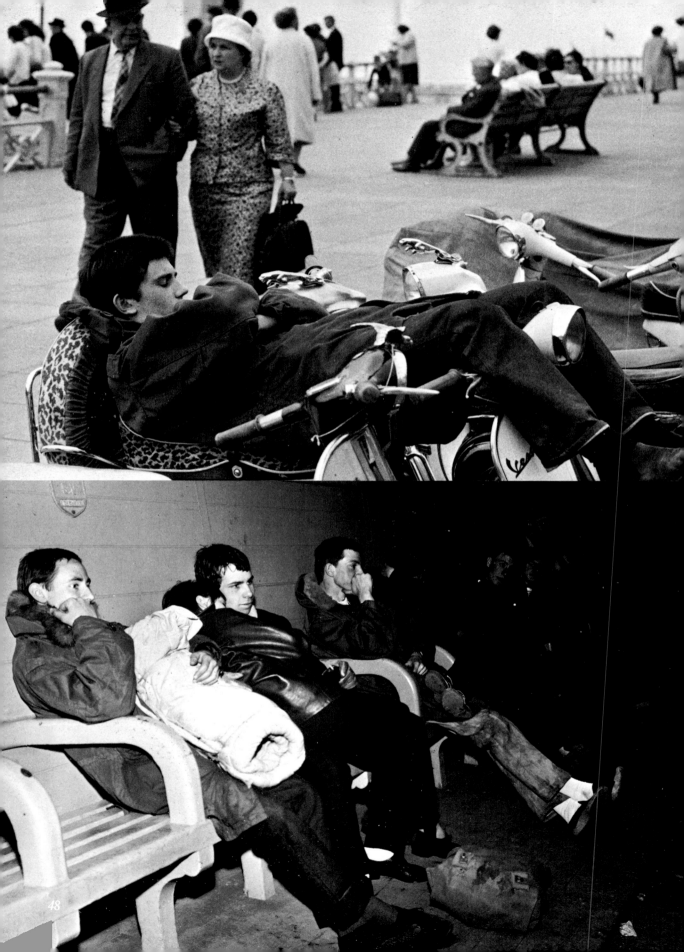

50

51

53

Every week there would be a new dance. They usually started at the 'Scene' club and then were demonstrated on 'Ready, Steady, Go'. The five shown here, accompanied by a brief guide to their movements, were among the most important dances of that period.

1. The Block *Crouch down, arms slightly bent, palms facing floor. Place one foot very quickly in front of the other, twisting heel as it lands. Spin round on back of heels, improvising intricate footwork. Tommy Tucker's 'Hi Heel Sneekers' is good to dance to it.*

2. The Hitch Hike *Place feet firmly, knees slightly bent, shake hips. Place hands at side, thumbs pointing up. Alternatively jerk arms over shoulders, then both arms over one shoulder, and occasionally jump to either side. Danced to the 'Hitch Hike' by Russell Byrd.*

3. The Shake *Stand firmly with one foot forward, arms stretched out, swing from side to side, nod the head. Shake the body from the hips and occasionally jump to the left or right. The Isley Brothers 'Twist & Shout' is a good 'shake' record.*

4. The Dog *Crouch down with feet slightly apart, arms slightly bent. Jerk body and arms backwards and forewards to the rhythm. Then jerk clenched hands over alternate shoulders. Jump to the left or right. It's perfect to dance to 'Do the Dog' by Rufus Thomas.*

5. The Ska *Crouch down swaying the hips from side to side while 'milking a cow' with the hands. At the same time move slowly up and down, occasionally lifting one leg up high. A typical Ska record is 'Jamaica Ska' by the Ska Kings.*

AQUARIUM

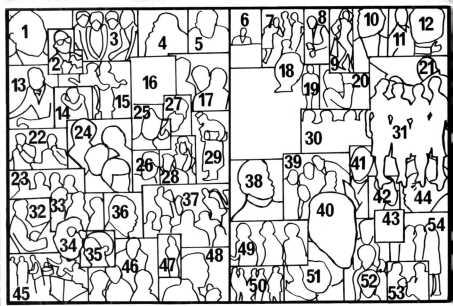

1. Rufus Thomas.
2. Little Stevie Wonder.
3. The Crystals.
4. Ben E. King.
5. Joe Tex.
6. Georgie Fame.
7. The Marvellettes.
8. Chris Farlowe and the Thunderbirds.
9. Ike and Tina Turner.
10. Mose Allison.
11. Sam Cooke.
12. John Lee Hooker.
13. Wilson Pickett.
14. Arthur Conley.
15. The Soul Sisters.
16. Booker T and the MG's.
17. Jimmy James and the Vagabonds.
18. Fontella Bass.
19. Eddie Floyd.
20. James Brown.
21. Billy Stewart.
22. Bob and Earl.
23. Smokey Robinson and the Miracles.
24. The Chiffons.
25. Dionne Warwick.
26. Aretha Franklin.
27. Ketty Lester.
28. Inez and Charlie Foxx.
29. Prince Buster.
30. The Four Tops.
31. The Shirelles.
32. Chuck Berry.
33. The Shangri-Las.
34. Ray Charles.
35. Laverne Baker.
36. Otis Redding.
37. Geno Washington and the RamJam Band.
38. Herbie Goins and the Night Timers.
39. The Temptations.
40. Marvin Gaye.
41. Lee Dorsey.
42. Don Covay.
43. Doris Troy.
44. Percey Sledge.
45. Zoot Money and the Big Roll Band.
46. Gladys Knight and the Pips.
47. Sugar Pie Di Santo.
48. Jimmy Cliff.
49. Martha and the Vandellas.
50. The Drifters.
51. Mary Wells.
52. The Ronnettes.
53. Sam and Dave.
54. The Supremes.

Key to p.74 & 75

The biggest rave name i

GEORGI
FAME
with th
BLUE FLAM

His 1st single released Jan.

'do the dog

Flipside: 'SHOP AROUND'

From the L.P.
'GEORGIE FAME
at the
FLAMINGO'

mono

75

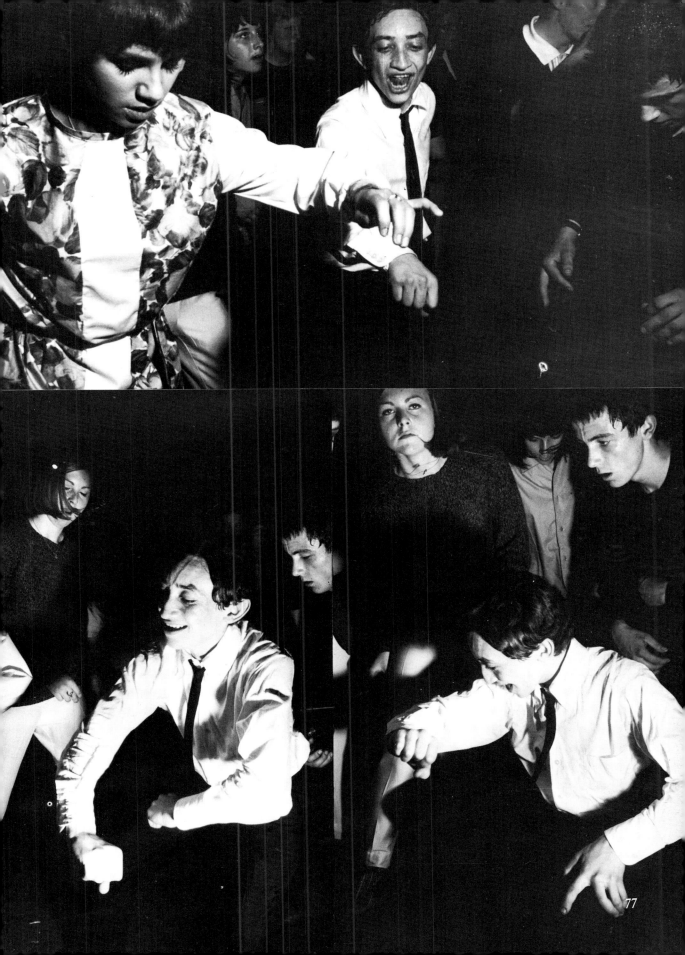

ATLANTIC
45 RPM
58/674
Under licence from Atlantic Recording Corp., U.S.A.
LAST NIGHT
(The Mar-Keys)
THE MAR-KEYS
POLYDOR RECORDS LIMITED

CHESS
45 R.P.M.
CRS 8025
DO I MAKE MYSELF CLEAR
(Dotkal & Fortune)
ETTA JAMES & SUGAR PIE DeSANTO
Produced by Billy Davis

CAMEO—PARKWAY
45 RPM
DON'T HANG UP
THE ORLONS

LONDON
AMERICAN RECORDINGS
MADE IN ENGLAND
45 R.P.M
HLU 9687
RECORDING FIRST PUBLISHED 1963
Recorded by DIMENSION, New York
BIEM/NCB
C. Bem, MCPS
Aldon Music Ltd.
LET'S TURKEY TROT
(Goffin, King)
LITTLE EVA

Stateside
45 RPM
SS 203
Tollie Music Ltd.
45KR-4109
A "Vee Jay" Recording
BOOM BOOM
(J. Hooker)
JOHN LEE HOOKER
E.M.I. RECORDS LIMITED

YOU CAN'T SIT DOWN
Part One
(Clark—Upchurch—Muldrow)
Time: 2.40
45 R.P.M.
Boyd Records USA
Sue RECORDS
WI-4005 (A)
PHIL UPCHURCH COMBO
Produced by Bobby Boyd

LONDON
AMERICAN RECORDINGS
MADE IN ENGLAND
45 R.P.M
45-HLU 9634
RECORDING FIRST PUBLISHED 1963
Recorded by DIMENSION, New York
Aldon Music Ltd.
CHAINS
(Goffin, King)
THE COOKIES

Stateside
45 RPM
SS 485
Ardmore & Beechwood Ltd.
45KR-4621
An Amy Mala Recording
SOLD IN U.K. SUBJECT TO RESALE PRICE CONDITIONS SEE PRICE LISTS
GET OUT OF MY LIFE, WOMAN
(Allen Toussaint)
LEE DORSEY
Produced by Tou-Sea Productions for Marshall E. Sehorn Prods.
E.M.I. RECORDS LIMITED

YOU CAN PUSH IT (OR PULL IT)
(Dallas—Elbert—Cevetello)
Time: 2.37
Sue RECORDS
WI-396 (A)
DONNIE ELBERT

LONDON
AMERICAN RECORDINGS
ATLANTIC
45 r.p.m.
HLK 9724
RECORDING FIRST PUBLISHED 1963
K/T
McLaughlin
HELLO STRANGER
(Lewis)
BARBARA LEWIS

Stateside
45 RPM
SS 307
Belinda (London) BIEM
45KR-4315
A Tamla-Motown Prod.
SOLD IN U.K. SUBJECT TO RESALE PRICE CONDITIONS SEE PRICE LISTS
Recording first published 1964
EVERY LITTLE BIT HURTS
(Ed Cobb)
BRENDA HOLLOWAY
Producers Davis & Gordon
E.M.I. RECORDS LIMITED

ALL ABOUT MY GIRL
Saturn Music
Sue RECORDS
WI-303
JIMMY McGRIFF

ATLANTIC
45 R.P.M
AT.4050
MADE IN ENGLAND BY THE DECCA RECORD CO. LTD UNDER LICENCE FROM ATLANTIC
© 1965
K/T
Belinda M. Ltd.
GEMA
BIEM
MSM 7362
MY GIRL
(Robinson, White)
OTIS REDDING

JUMP UP
ISLAND RECORDS LIMITED
45 R.P.M.
MADE IN ENGLAND
JU-511 (511 A)
© 1963
Copyright Control Telco Records
DR. KITCH
Lord Kitchener

BLUE BEAT
45 R.P.M
45/BB 30 (45/BB 30-A)
A "Buster" Recording Copyright Control
CAROLINA
(Abrahams)
THE FOLKS BROTHERS
Count Ossie Afro-Combo
MELODISC RECORDS LTD.

LONDON
AMERICAN RECORDINGS
MADE IN ENGLAND
45 R.P.M
45-HL 9581
RECORDING FIRST PUBLISHED 1962
Produced by Jerry Goffin for Dimension Records, New York
Aldon Music
THE LOCO-MOTION
(Goffin, King)
LITTLE EVA

PYE INTERNATIONAL
45 RPM
7N.25241
SEVENTEEN SAVILE ROW
1.45 (241 A)
RECORDING FIRST PUBLISHED 1964
45KR-4048
WALK ON BY
(B. Bacharach)
DIONNE WARWICK
Arranged and Conducted by Burt Bacharach
A Scepter, U.S.A. Recording

TOP RANK
45-JAR 132
KANSAS CITY
(Stoller—Leiber)
2.21
RECORDING FIRST PUBLISHED 1959
A 'FURY' Recording
WILBERT HARRISON
Macmelodies

LONDON
AMERICAN RECORDINGS
MADE IN ENGLAND
45 R.P.M
HLU 9773
RECORDING FIRST PUBLISHED 1963
K/T
Recorded by PHILLES, Hollywood
NCB
57 Savile Row
THEN HE KISSED ME
(Spector, Greenwich, Barry)
THE CRYSTALS

Stateside
45 RPM
SS 163
Roosevelt Ltd.
Meenloo
45KR-4027
A "Loen" Recording
LET'S STOMP
(Goldstein—Feldman—Gottehrer)
BOBBY COMSTOCK
E.M.I. RECORDS LIMITED

Stateside
45 RPM
SS 181
Aldon Music Ltd.
C. Bem
BIEM/NCB
45KR-4063
A "Scepter" Recording
FOOLISH LITTLE GIRL
(Helen Miller—Howard Greenfield)
THE SHIRELLES
A Stan Green Prod.
A Luda Prod.
E.M.I. RECORDS LIMITED

COLPIX RECORDS
43 RPM
PX.11010-A
EDWIN H. MORRIS
PX 11010
RECORDING FIRST PUBLISHED 1963
SWINGING ON A STAR (Van Heusen, Burke)
BIG DEE IRWIN
Produced by Gerry Goffin
A Dimension, U.S.A. Recording

ATLANTIC
45 R.P.M
AT.4015
MADE IN ENGLAND BY THE DECCA RECORD CO. LTD UNDER LICENCE FROM ATLANTIC RECORD CO. INC.
K/T
© 1964
Burlington Music
HOLD WHAT YOU'VE GOT
(Tex)
JOE TEX

SEND FOR ME
Saturn Music
Sue
WI-316 A
(BR 1056)
BARBARA GEORGE

DANCER
GO

THE MOODY BLUES
BOSS
R&B
SUNDAY OCT 4th
7.30-11

aramore ballroom
ballham high rd

s·scene

MEMBERSHIP CARD
THE CONCHORDS
Sunday Club
★ ★
THE WHITE HART :: SOUTHALL
7.00 p.m. to 10.30 p.m.

Name *J.M. Knows*

DANCER
3rd July
1964

Flamingo & Allnighter Clubs
33-37 WARDOUR STREET, LONDON. W.I.
Office GER 8251 — Club GER 1549

MEMBERSHIP   CARD

on their first disc outing,
four hip young men
from london say:

i'm the face
and wear:
zoot suit

(the first authentic mod record)

the four hip young men?

the high numbers

fontana tf 480
release date july 3rd 1964

KLOOKS KLEEK DECEMBER PROGRAMME

MONDAYS IN DECEMBER
Dec. 7th ... John Mayall's Bluesbreakers (Special Decca Recording Session)   3/6
.. 14th ... From the U.S.A. we present a great Blues Session HOWLING WOLF and HUBERT SUMLIN with the T-Bones plus the Blueknights   6/6
.. 21st ... Zoot Money's Big Roll Band   3/6
.. 28th ... John Mayall's Bluesbreakers   3/6

TUESDAYS IN DECEMBER
Dec. 1st   The Art Woods   4/-
.. 8th   Graham Bond Organisation   4/-
.. 15th   Chris Farlowe and The Thunderbirds   4/-
.. 22nd   KLOOKS KRISTMAS PARTY with Ronnie Jones and the Night-Timers (full details to be announced later)   4/-
.. 29th   Alexis Korner's Blues Inc.   4/-

STOP PRESS
FOR ONE WEDNESDAY ONLY   Dec. 16th
we proudly present
RUFUS THOMAS with The Chessmen   7/6

MARQUEE CLUB
| | AUGUST 1964 NEWSLETTER |

NATIONAL JAZZ FEDERATION, 18, CARLISLE STREET, LONDON, W.I GER 8923
JAZZ AND BLUES FESTIVAL 1964

MEMBERSHIP

4th NATIONAL JAZZ & BLUES FESTIVAL — RICHMOND

7.30-10	**FRIDAY, 7th AUGUST**	Tickets 10/-
	Rhythm and Blues	
	THE ROLLING STONES	
	THE T-BONES THE AUTHENTICS THE GREBELS, ETC.	
2-5.30	**SATURDAY, 8th AUGUST**	Tickets 5/-
	Modern Jazz	
	RONNIE SCOTT QUARTET JOHNNY	
	SCOTT QUINTET DICK MORRISSEY QUARTET	
	TUBBY HAYES BIG BAND	
6.30-11.30	Blues and Jazz	
	CHRIS BARBER BAND OTTILIE PATTERSON	
	ALEX WELSH BAND COLIN KINGWELL BAND LONG	
	JOHN BALDRY AND THE HOOCHIE COOCHIE MEN	
	MANFRED MANN, also American Stars	
All-day Tickets 12/6	**MEMPHIS SLIM and JIMMY WITHERSPOON**	
1-5.30	**SUNDAY, 9th AUGUST**	Tickets 10/-
	National Amateur Jazz Contest	
	FINAL HEATS FOR 14 BANDS OF ALL STYLES CHOSEN FROM	
	CONTESTS ALL OVER BRITAIN AND AWARD OF THE GUARDS	
	TROPHIES	
6.30-11.30	Jazz and Rhythm & Blues	Tickets 10/-
	KENNY BALL BAND AFRICAN MESSENGERS	
	GRAHAM BOND GROUP HUMPHREY LYTTELTON BAND	
	GEORGIE FAME and the BLUE FLAMES also the	
All-day Tickets 12/6	YARDBIRDS and American Star	
	MOSE ALLISON	
	WEEKEND TICKETS 20/- IN ADVANCE	

TO: NATIONAL JAZZ FESTIVAL BOOKING DEPT.

4th NATIONAL JAZZ FESTIVAL AUG. 7.8.9.
ATHLETIC ASSOCIATION GROUNDS
RICHMOND, SURREY

-Motown Appreciation Society
9 Church Road, Bexleyheath, Kent
M E M B E R

THE HIGH NUMBERS
EVERY TUESDAY 3/6
RAILWAY HOTEL HARROW & WEALDSTONE !

NEXT WEEK AT TILES!
1st - 6th March

TUESDAY	RADIO LUXEMBOURG'S 'Ready Steady Radio'	IN TILES SHOPPING ARCADE
WEDNESDAY	THE EVENING NEWS' 'Young London Spins' DISC SESSION	
THURSDAY	The Alan Price Set THE SYMBOLS	LATE NIGHT SHOPPING EVERY NIGHT
FRIDAY	Clarence 'Frogman' Henry THE KOOBAS THE CHECKMATES	
SATURDAY	The Riot Squad EVERETT OF ENGLAND and TOP SUPPORTING GROUPS	
SUNDAY	Ted Heath Swing Session THE TED HEATH ORCHESTRA	THE ARCADE OPENS AT 6 p.m. NIGHTLY

NEXT WEEK AT 79 Oxford Street!
Entrance at No. 1 Dean Street
Membership Application Forms are available at the door.   1966 Membership 7/-

BLAISE'S
Blaise's Club 121 Queens Gate SW7 KEN 62

READY STEADY'S PENULTIMATE

The last programme for Ready Steady Goer's
ill be on THURSDAY DECEMBER 16.

you would like to be on this show, with
uest, then please fill in the attached
return it to me by Friday November 19.

READY STEADY GO!

N°   318

FILLES

1	2	
R'N'B	R'N'B	MOD

AS FROM
MONDAY, 13th APRIL
KLOOKS KLEEK
STARTS MONDAY
RHYTHM 'N' BLUES
SESSIONS
SAME PRICE !   SAME BAN
2 BANDS EVERY SESSION
AND NOT RECORDS DURING THE INTER
So . . . . Make a Date at 8
on Monday, 13th April fo
GEORGIE FAME
3/6

ADY
TEADY
O!

EADY, GO!
SEPTEMBER 1965
Reception Desk, The
Studios, Empire Way,
wing gum, smoking or

RUSION
✸
REDIFFUSION
LONDON
TWO

YOU HAVE BEEN CHOSEN TO DANCE ON

Recording - TUESDAYS 6.15 to 7.00 p.m.
of RSG   Doors open 5.45 to 6.00 p.m.
REDIFFUSION TELEVISION STUDIOS
EMPIRE WAY
WEMBLEY
No admittance under 16 years
for conditions see back

READY STEADY GO!

FRIDAY, SEPT. 16th AT TILES!
First Time in the U.K. the FABULOUS
OTIS REDDING
with his 11 Piece All American Band

IN TILES
SHOPPING
ARCADE
LATE NIGHT
SHOPPING
EVERY
NIGHT !

TWO COMPLETE SHOWS
FIRST SHOW 9.30 p.m.
SECOND SHOW 12.30 a.m.

LATE NIGHT TWO PERFORMANCE TICKETS   20 - 25 -
LATE NIGHT SHOW ONLY   15 - 17.6

Radio Luxembourg
208 LUNCHTIME
DISC PARTIES

1 - Entrance

CLEM DALTON

79 OXFORD STREET

go Vespa

DMIT
E

85

SUPER SPORT

105 km.h   Vespa   **65,3** m.p.h

Vespa G.S.

paradiso per due

magazine MIRROR

INSIDE THE MIND OF A MOD

SHE is seventeen years old and she said: "My name is Teresa, but I like to be called Terry, please."

She was very polite and nice and she looked younger than seventeen.

She wore tight, black stretch pants, striped socks, flat canvas laced-up sneakers, a white cotton T-shirt and a blue suede jacket..

Her dark hair was short and rough. She wore no make-up except around her eyes and not really much there. Her eyebrows were plucked to a thin line.

She appears to be, you would agree if you met her, a perfectly ordinary inoffensive sort of teen-age girl.

SHE IS A MOD.

I had never, actually come up against one at very close quarters, being I suppose what they would call utterly square and old (anyone over twenty-four is old).

I am square enough to think deck chairs are for sitting in and milk bottles are for milk and have never regarded either of them as offensive weapons.

AFTER talking to Terry Gordon, yesterday, I realise how uneducated I am.

Terry kindly took it upon herself to teach me the facts of Mod and Rocker life, and taking the view that you can never learn too much. I listened attentively.

She began by defining the basic differences between Mods and Rockers And Statics.

I had never come across a State and wondered what kind of breed *that* was. Terry told me. . . .

● A State is a person who thinks he (or she) is a Mod. They go around saying they are Mods, but they don't really know what a Mod is.

● A State is neither one thing (or another—a phoney, really.

You've got to be either a Mod or a Rocker to mean anything. Mods are neat and clean. They have cropped hair. Rockers have long hair.

Rocker girls do up their hair kind of high and it's all stiff and lacquered.

Rocker boys wear it long and greasy like Elvis Presley, only worse.

Mod girls don't wear any make-up—only the eyes and maybe foundation. Rocker girls use a lot of bright pink lipstick and piles of make-up.

Mods (both sexes) wear stretch pants and sneakers and tee-shirts with large initials sewn on, maybe their own or USA. Some Mod girls wear skirts to just below the knee.

In the summer we'll wear white pants and so will Mod boys. Blue-beat skirts are out.

Rocker girls wear ordinary sweaters and very short tight skirts, dark stockings and winkle-picker shoes.

Rocker boys wear leather gear and jeans with studs and fancy boots with heels.

Mod girls wear small earrings. Rocker girls wear long dangling ones.

Rockers are the minority group: about 25 per cent. Rockers to Mods ●

CAREFULLY I listened to all this and said I thought I would now be able to tell the difference if I was careless enough to be spending a week-end at the seaside in a deckchair during a Mod-Rocker invasion.

It is a pity, in a way, we can't just hand over a few old deck chairs and a deserted chunk of Brighton beach and seal it off and let them play their ridiculous kids' games so we could snooze in the sun in peace.. But they wouldn't care for that.

I said to Terry: "Mods and Rockers are exhibitionists, aren't they?"

She said, this honest child: "We need someone to take notice of us and fighting is a way of attracting attention. The word gets around and it gets exciting and you go where you think the fights are going to be. But not all of us take part in the fighting. I don't."

I said: "What are they actually fighting about? Do you know?"

She said: "The Mods want to get rid of the Rockers. We hate and despise them. They can join us if they like."

She paused and then she said, grimly: "Or they can get out of the country."

I said: "Isn't there room for all of you? You are so intolerant."

She said: "Yes, we are. They've got a different attitude to life. Mods enjoy life. They like to dance. Rockers don't dance.

"Mods like blues and blue beat rhythm music and they go to clubs and dance. Rockers just listen to pop music.

"I belong to three Mod clubs. One I go to a lot is called The Last Chance. It's a kind of saloon with swinging doors and they have rope nooses for decoration.

"We drink coke or coffee. Rockers carry knives. Mods don't have weapons."

"Only deckchairs," I said. "And milk bottles." She nodded.

SHE said: "People like the clubs. They stay there all night, some of them. I don't ever. They take Purple Hearts to keep awake and Bombers. A Bomber is equivalent to twelve hearts.

"They take them to keep awake and to have confidence. The price has gone up recently.

"Hearts cost about ninepence each now. I have never taken any. I am frightened to. They say girls who take them won't be able to have any babies and they harm your body.

"I want to get married sometime and have bab-

ies—after I've travelled and seen the world."

She'd better, I thought, keep out of the way of flick knives and broken deck chairs or her ambitions may never be realised.

TERRY Gordon, at seventeen, is still at school.

She gets £2 a week pocket money which she spends on Mod clubs, on Mod clothes and on Mod seaside excursions.

She is your child. And mine. What are we going to do about her? Laugh? Weep? Shrug indifferently and put it all down to high-spirited youth in need of an outlet?

Terry Gordon says they'll all grow out of it, she thinks. When they've got rid of the Rockers.

It's like nursery stuff, really. Cops and robbers. Or cowboys and Indians.

If only it wasn't for the blood and the pills and the broken windows and disturbing peaceful seaside weekends, I'd be in favour of just leaving them alone to fight it out.

THEY'LL GET AS BORED WITH IT ALL IN THE END AS I AM WITH THEM, ALREADY.

Terry Gordon, a 17-year-old Mod.

After the tumult of Margate and Brighton, MARJORIE PROOPS takes a deep look at one girl's thinking

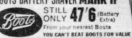

91

Sunday Mirror

6d. May 31, 1964 No. 61

EXPOSING THE DRUG MENACE

A SUNDAY MIRROR WARNING TO PARENTS

By Norman Lucas and Victor Sims

A SHOCK report on the spread of drug-taking among young people has been passed by Scotland Yard's Drug Squad to the Metropolitan Police Commissioner, Sir Joseph Simpson.

A nationwide check reveals that nearly 10,000 teenagers are buying pep-pills and narcotics on the black market.

London's West End is named as the centre of this disturbing growth in the nation's drug problem, with Liverpool, Cardiff, Birmingham and Glasgow as other black spots.

The report says that unless strong action is taken soon the drug-habit among youngsters will swell to even greater proportions.

In their fight to stamp it out both the Yard and provincial police forces want to enlist the aid of parents.

Inquiries in London and the Provinces make one thing clear: too many parents are showing an alarming indifference to the fact that their children may become drug addicts.

Fertile Ground

Some parents are unaware that their sons and daughters are pouring into large towns in groups to spend week-ends in all-night clubs and dives.

In these places—fertile ground for drug-pedlars—their children can, within weeks, become slaves to narcotics. They begin by experimenting with purple hearts and other pep-pills, then progress via "reefers" (marijuana) to heroin and cocaine—the two drugs that almost always lead to death before the age of thirty-five.

Look how serious the position has become:

● SO MANY thefts have taken place from vans carrying supplies of drugs from the makers to the wholesalers that police have introduced special

Continued on Page 2

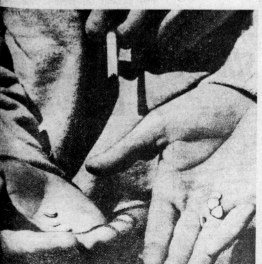

Purple heart tablets . . in the hands of teenagers they can bring disaster.

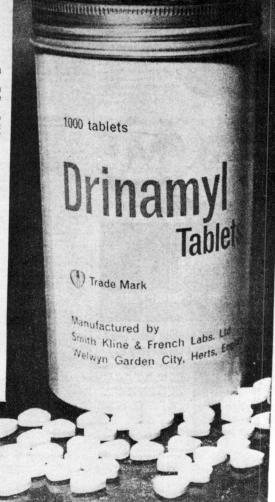

1000 tablets

Drinamyl Tablets

Ⓤ Trade Mark

Manufactured by Smith Kline & French Labs. Ltd Welwyn Garden City, Herts, Eng

The container above holds 1,000 purple heart tablets. If you find a container like it, tell the police.

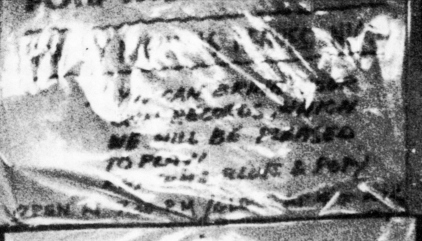

£50 REWARD!

THE MANAGMENT WILL PAY £50 TO ANY PERSON WHO CAN PROVIDE CONCRETE EVIDENCE DIRECT TO THE POLICE [REG 1113] THAT ANY MEMBER OF THE MANAGMENT OF THE DISCOTHEQUE CLUB IS RESPONSIBLE FOR THE SALE OF

PURPLE HEARTS

THE COMMITTEE

Sunday Mirror EXPOSING THE DRUG MENACE

ONE NIGHT 1,000

**Report by Sunday Mirror Investigators
RONALD MAXWELL and LYNN LEWIS**

WE found Swiss Albert at four o'clock in the morning. The man called "faceless" in the Commons last week, and named as front man of "a notorious centre for drug addiction," La Discotheque Club, had just finished his night's work among London teenagers.

He was carrying a morning paper when he arrived at the Earls Court rooming house. We were carrying 1,000 "Purple Heart" pills bought a few hours earlier from a Discotheque member.

We also had in our pockets some reefers —marijuana cigarettes — bought inside the Flamingo Club, Wardour-street, and some capsule drugs known as "black and greens" bought in the Desiree Coffee Bar, Soho.

We wanted to talk to Swiss Albert, known officially as Mr. Albert Grew, about the drug generation and to hear his side of an extraordinary story of a mystery management controlling his and other clubs.

But Swiss Albert, a thin, weedy man in grey, his eyes distorted by thick pebble glasses, seems voiceless as well as "faceless."

Broken Promise

"I am not talking without my lawyer," he said. Then he promised to phone us a few hours later to arrange a meeting in the presence of his lawyer.

"I won't fail," he assured us

Swiss Albert has not telephoned. So his lawyer must have advised him not to discuss with us the facts which have emerged from our day-and-night inquiries into drugs and clubs in Soho, or the allegations about him and his club made by Mr. Ben Parkin, Labour M P for Paddington North, in Parliament on Tuesday

It is a pity Swiss Albert cannot talk—a pity for every misled youngster ruining life and health and future with drugs bought at places like Mr. Grew's club.

Concession Money?

We felt sure that an honourable man, advised by a solicitor, would consider it his public duty to help end racketeering and teenage drug-taking if he could. We would like to ask Mr. Grew this question:

Does La Discotheque draw "concession money" from people who sell drugs illegally on the premises?

We have evidence that drugs like Purple Hearts are sold on the premises by young men and even girls who are club members.

And in the Commons last week Mr. Parkin said, during the committee debate

The three doors to temptation

on the Drugs (Prevention of Misuse) Bill :

"We already know that the racket in Purple Hearts has been so arranged that the beneficial owners [of the club] are no longer personally concerned because they have sold it off in concessions."

Mr. Parkin explained that in club organisation it was common for the bar and cloakroom to be "let" to someone willing to pay a good rent to the club owner.

Once this is done "the chap is allowed to sell Purple Hearts as long as it is not brought to the attention of the authorities. It is at his risk, and he pays extra for the concession."

Geared For Young Ones

We went to Soho to find out how widespread the sale of drugs is in the clubs. The first thing we discovered was that drugs are for young people only.

The most notorious clubs are so geared for the younger generation that anyone much over twenty is as welcome as a Rocker at a Mod party.

Nobody sells anything to people who are the wrong age or wearing the wrong clothes.

We arranged with two teenagers to buy drugs for us. One was an addict taking between thirty and forty pills a day The other took pills for kicks for two years, but stopped with medical help earlier this year.

Both named La Discotheque, in Wardour-street, as the best place to start. We searched them before they went in to make sure they started out without drugs.

Five minutes later they returned and said they could find no one inside carrying pills because of "the scare" caused by Mr. Parkin. But in the club they had met a member

THE FLAMINGO
From this club we were brought reefers—5s. each.

LA DISCOTHEQUE
Here a deal was [made] for the "Purple Hea[rts"]

Who runs clubs?

and arranged to see him half-an-hour later to buy 1,000 Purple Hearts for £18.

That worked out at just over 4d. each — cheap because of the bulk buying. Normally young addicts pay a shilling a pill, and buy about ten at a time.

As there was time to kill before "the meet" one youngster went to the Flamingo Club, just a few doors away in Wardour-street.

He returned quickly with two reefers, or marijuana cigarettes, known to the drug generation of today as "splits." They cost five shillings each and were clumsily hand-made.

The other youngster went

to the Desiree Coffee Bar, near Frith-street. He came out apologetically and said that all he had been able to get were " black and greens" and they had cost two shillings each. He said he bought only nine.

These capsules were identified as Librium, a tranquilliser. An overdose taken with alcohol could release inhibitions.

A few minutes after these deals were completed the youngsters met their drug-contact from La Discotheque. He told them he had now arranged to pick up the pills and would return in ten minutes. He left in a taxi.

It was twelve minutes

before the taxi retu[rned] Both youths got in[to it] and completed the [deal] while the taxi tra[velled] round the block.

They returned to us [with] four envelopes, each f[ull of] pills.

"It's best to do [the] deal in a taxi," one [of] them explained. "[It's] easier to examine [what] you're buying [and] nobody can see you."

They also explained [that] the pills were not th[e real] Purple Hearts. [These] ones, we were told by [the] youths and others, are [not] obtainable at the mo[ment] so young addicts buy [other] drugs.

But they still refe[r...]

VE BOUGHT PURPLE EARTS'

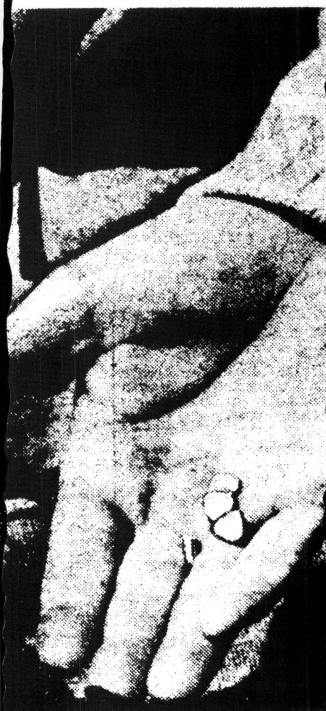

DESIREE
COFFEE BAR

DESIREE

Tranquilliser capsules came from here at a cost of 2s. each.

Purple Hearts, or " blues," as they had bought and were identi- as amphetamine a pep pill. Large these and similar t takers such a t they dance all out rest.

young addicts e swollen feet ht for us were ght hours of jazz sing.

tor told us: "The ake them go on the normal limits rance. It strains arts as well as t."

the taxi-ride on, the pills that ht for us were genuine. Some aspirin were mixed in with the hundreds of pep pills.

They looked almost identical, but the pep pills had a groove running across one side.

This sort of swindling is common. And the sucker can't complain.

One young man boasted to us that he had sold glu-cose tablets at a shilling each to kick-hunting kids from the provinces who did not know their way around.

It is almost impossible to walk through Soho late at night without being made aware of the drug traffic.

At 2 a.m. in Old Compton - street, a couple of pretty teenage girls swayed up to us singing:

" Don't take those purple
pills, my love.
In the end they'll make
you blue.
If you take those purple
pills, my love
Black death will dance
with you."

Lionel Blake, 26-year-old boss of the Scene Club, told us: "It's almost im-possible to stop people selling pills in clubs, even for those of us who really try.

" If I find anybody sell-ing drugs I bounce him hard, but it still seems to go on a little.

" It is not always the club-owner's fault that drugs are sold on his premises."

The Second Question

The owner of La Discotheque might share that view. But who is the owner?

That is the second ques-tion we would like to ask the voiceless, faceless pos-sibly harmless, Mr. Grew.

Mr. Parkin told the Com-mons on Tuesday: The owner of La Discotheque would be able to prove he did not own it. I was amused the gentleman with the 80 per cent. shareholding was the ubiquitous and faceless Albert Grew, known as Swiss Albert.

" Grew is the most honest of men, quite happy to go on earning £20 a week from his master, and to whom one can entrust any property. So his name occurs again and again.

" Give it to Swiss Albert and he will give it back to you on Thursday if you say that he should.

A third question we

would like to put to Mr. Grew is: Why does La Discotheque, a club for youngsters, have so many strong-arm men at the door?

Is it to protect the club from gangsters?

Some clubmen we have talked to are worried that the profitable drug busi-ness centred in Soho is attracting more crooks than ever to the district, and that gangsterism is increasing.

There are particularly worried about an organisation which some people call " The Peace-makers."

It is said to be bossed by a well-dressed man who lives lavishly in the same road as a Cabinet Minister and who always carries a red - handled, hand - made " Derringer " in his waist-coat pocket. It fires a single 0.22 bullet.

The Peacemakers operate a protection racket by offering part-time bouncers and bodyguards to club owners. The service is ex-pensive.

In fact it is usually a proportion of the takings. Anyone who refuses the service, however, starts having trouble and fights in his club shortly after-wards.

The head of the Peace-makers is claimed by some to be the most powerful man in Soho.

Favourite Weapon

Blackmail is said to be a favourite weapon of the boss of the Peacemakers.

He uses tape-recorded in-discretions to force people to perform services for him.

Some of his victims are drug addicts, often respect-able people afraid that their weakness will be dis-closed to employers or families.

Drug-taking always attracts gangsters. They like the huge profits.

Tablets worth about 5s. a hundred are sold at £5 a hundred. They also like to exploit human weakness in other ways.

Many girls have been led into prostitution by drug-taking. Their immoral earnings pay for their illegal kicks.

In Parliament Mr. Parkin even quoted the case of a 16-year-old drug addict who became a male prostitute to buy his drugs.

And today the Soho set-up is such that the same thing could hap-pen to anyone's child.

'Pusher' Confesses

A startling claim by a youth of twenty that he has been selling 1,000 " Purple Hearts " in thirty minutes is being probed by Scotland Yard.

The youth, a cured addict, walked into the Sunday Mirror and named six men who supply the pills to " pushers " in lots of 1,000 to sell for £25.

WHEN I ASKED FOR THE 'GEAR'..

By Madeleine Harmsworth

IT took me under ten minutes to buy sixty " Purple Hearts " for a shilling each in London's West End.

It was an ordinary, and frighteningly easy deal.

How was it done . . . ?

In and out of Soho's clubs and cafes a girl alone soon makes friends. I met Mick, and asked if

he had any " gear," an expression covering "smokes" (reefers), and "pills," "circles," or "blues" (Purple Hearts).

Mick took me to see Bob, 15. Then on to see Dave, 20. These two took me to Coco's, in Robert-street, St. Pancras.

There a customer took a packet from his belt. Carefully, he shook out

thirty pills. We handed over 30s.

Then into the Bamboo, off Tottenham Court road. Dave made our mission clear to a custo-mer. Quickly and silently, thirty pills were shaken into our hands for 30s.

Dave suddenly turned to me and said: " I think you're the law. Come on, Bob." They vanished.

teenagers they can bring disaster.

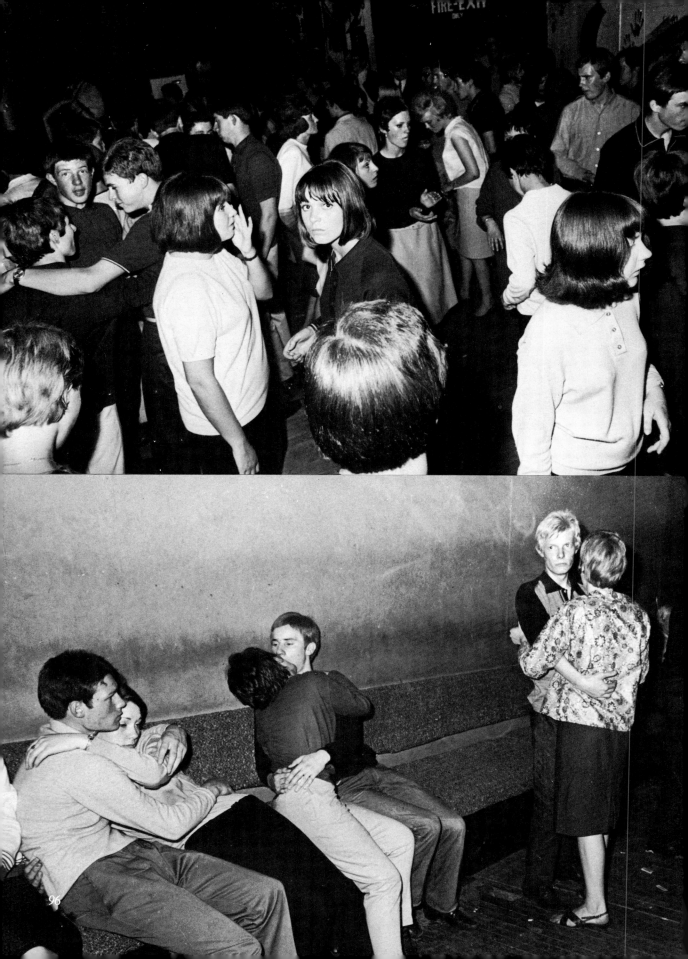

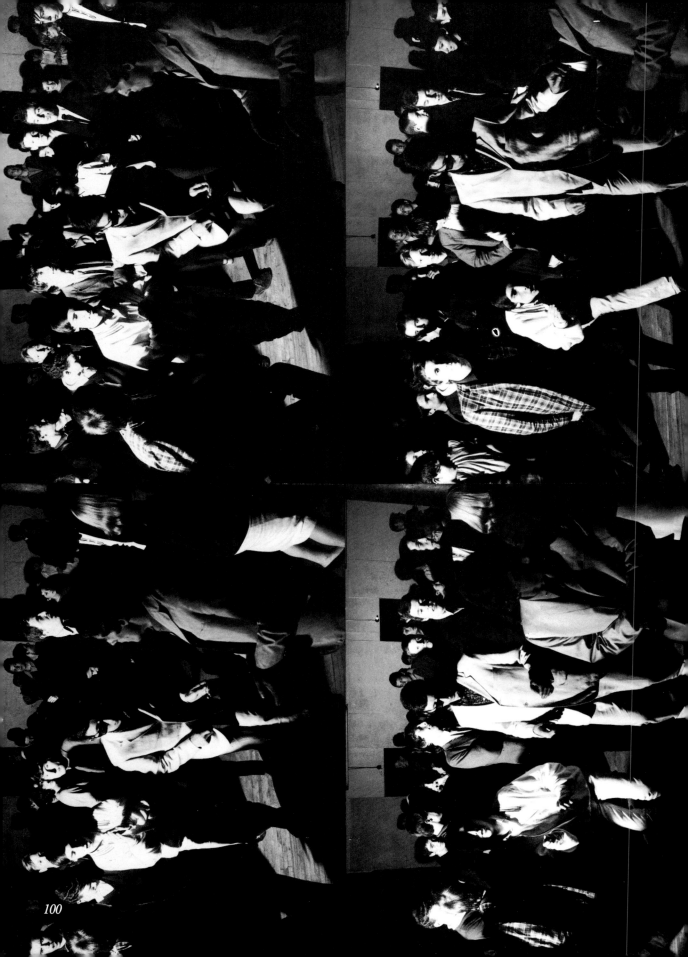

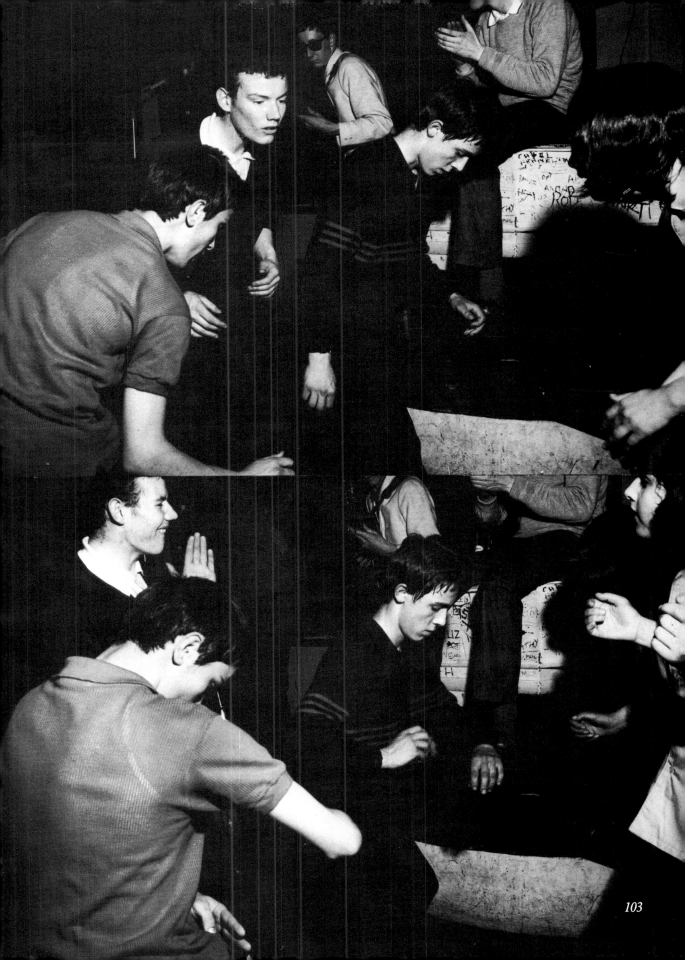

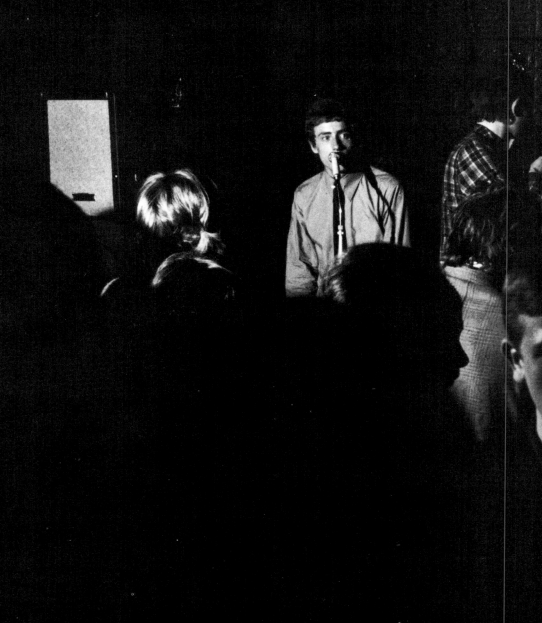

All on a
Summer's
Day

Wish you

IT'S SO NICE
THE BUSY CIT

were here!

Daily Mirror

Monday, March 30, 1964 • No. 18,746

Scooter gangs 'beat up' Clacton

'WILD ONES' INVADE SEASIDE—97 ARRESTS

By PAUL HUGHES

THE Wild Ones invaded a seaside town yesterday—1,000 fighting, drinking, roaring, rampaging teenagers on scooters and motor-cycles. By last night, after a day of riots and battles with police, ninety-seven of them had been arrested.

A desperate S O S went out from police at Clacton, Essex, as leather-jacketed youths and girls attacked people in the streets, turned over parked cars, broke into beach huts, smashed windows, and fought with rival gangs.

Police reinforcements from other Essex towns raced to the shattered resort, where fearful residents had locked themselves indoors.

By this time the centre of Clacton was jammed with screaming teenagers. Traffic was at a standstill.

Fought

The crowd was broken up as police and police dogs. Several policemen were injured as the teenagers fought them.

A number of arrests had already been made. Addresses had been taken, and messages sent to parents.

And worried mothers and fathers were beginning to arrive from the London area to haul out their sons and daughters.

The harassed police were glad to see them go. For the cells at Clacton police station were crammed with youngsters under arrest.

Its not just the scene of arrests and charges — and conscience — included.

Thirty-five assault on police and complaint there for creating disturbances and fighting were two further charges.

Twenty for other offences, including insulting words, malicious damage and using obscene language.

Rough

Police said the court sessions would begin on April 10.

The Wild Ones film was the title of a Marlon Brando film in which teenage motor-cyclists terrorised a town—later banned trouble in Clacton before. But not on this scale.

They began arriving on Friday and Saturday and many slept rough on the beach, under the pier, in promenade shelters, and in beach huts they broke into.

Others spent the night roaring round the town on their scooters and motor-cycles.

Waves

Earlier reports put the number of dead in the hundreds or even thousands.

Today Hugh Wade, Alaska's Secretary of State, said : "casualties are less than we ever dreamed they could be."

After the earthquake, which struck on Friday, giant waves travelling at a fantastic rate sped death and destruction as far as Crescent City, California, 1,300 miles away.

There are people died and between are missing. The tidal waves killing another six in California coastal towns and injured several more.

From the stricken Alaskan town of Anchorage Pop. 48,200 — a Mayor Communications

---

The Easter miracle of Alaska

'FEWER THAN 100' DIE

From BARRIE HARDING, New York, Sunday

THE earthquake which savaged Alaska is being described tonight as "The Easter Miracle."

For although the earthquake was one of the mightiest ever recorded, the loss of life throughout Alaska is an amazingly light hurry, with ninety-three injured.

Rescuers expect to find more bodies under the rubble of wrecked town.

But they estimate that the final death toll will be fewer than 100.

centre cabled last night—

A procession of U S Air Force planes are on the day with a sister to Alaska's five earthquake-shattered towns of Anchorage, Valdez, Seward, Whittier, and Kodiak.

They brought emergency Red Cross supplies, doctors, nurses and even a mobile hospital.

Meanwhile rescue workers were crawling through the bombed and hotel buildings of Anchorage looking for dead and injured.

A huge hole has been cleared out of the main street of the town and one side of the street has sunk 30ft, taking with it stores, a cinema, a restaurant, and small hotels.

Damage

Most of the fog-shrouded town is without heat, power, water or sewage facilities. Total damage is estimated at $573,000,000 and the townspeople are being warned to get typhoid injections.

Late tonight there were fears for the safety of eighteen small Eskimo villages along the Alaskan coast. Officials said they were not even sure whether the villages still existed.

On the shocked American pages that accompany Pictures—Pages FOUR and FIVE.

Youths in leather jackets help a policeman making inquiries last night during the rampage by gangs of teenagers at Clacton. A police dog stands by.

SUNDAY JOINT SAVED BY WIVES

There were no power cuts ... during the "Sunday lunch" yesterday.

The Central Electricity Generating Board said that rate was the prime reason for the success of the emergency appeal to housewives and others, not to use electrical appliances as much as possible.

Housewives were asked to turn off many electric points not in use.

A spokesman said : "Our magnificent

response to an appeal to housewives during the weekend contributed as little as possible to the nation-wide three-day bread, voltage reduction helped.

"Every kilowatt saved will conserve coal and help the Generating Board in the next few working days demand on Tuesday."

Leaders of the five unions involved in the Go-slow over pay and hours over the weekend began to decide whether to restore normal working—it not and overtime ban.

Last night a spokesman for the Power Workers Editorial Committee of the go-slow from over Britain—said :

"Demands are pouring in from the men to return leaders urging them to carry on the fight."

He added that "power workers throughout the country want to get a copy of copies to probe the dispute.

This was looked at he said, as an attempt to delay settlement of the problem.

Continued on Back Page

DAILY SKETCH

Tuesday, May 19, 1964 • Price Threepence • WEATHER: Early rain; sunny spells

Bensons FRUIT BONBONS ENJOY SOME TODAY!

bbing, stoning, deckchair battles as riots hit new peak

WILDEST ONES YET

MOMENT of frenzy as two Rockers leap 15 feet from the roof of Brighton Aquarium to escape from Mods wielding deck chairs.

Just part of the battle that raged in the town and took nearly 300 police to control.

At one point, as mobs of Mods chased isolated Rockers across the beach, families formed "wagon train" circles with their deck chairs to keep them out.

More pictures of Brighton riots: Pages 6—7.

Holidaymakers cower on the beach

Sketch Reporters

THE Wild Ones of Whitsun went even wilder yesterday—with two beach resort—especially at Margate.

Stabbings, attacks on police and violent clashes between Mods and Rockers, Holidaymakers cowered in their deck

chairs as the rampage spread from Margate to other South coast resort—especially Brighton.

The stabbings happened at Margate.

On the beach

THE FIRST man to be stabbed — in agony — appeared on the beach at Margate.

Two men approached the man at Margate, who lay standing on the

fringe of a 200-strong mob of "Mods."

"You are the bloke who stabbed him," said one. One of them punched him on the face. The other fired a starting pistol two inches from his eye.

White-faced, the man dumped as he was stabbed in his right arm.

His two attackers disappeared into the crowd.

Preston staggered across the road with blood pouring from his side and one. He shouted: "I've been stabbed."

Police bundled him into a Land Rover.

White-faced and shaken. He told one : "I don't know them. I don't know who happened."

First aid post

He was taken to Margate Hospital and released after antibiotic treatment.

THE SECOND STAB took place five minutes later near the clock tower on the sea front.

A battle began among a group of teenagers.

One screaming patron was bashed over the head with a beer bottle. Blood streaming from him as he slumped to the ground.

He, too, was released after antibiotic treatment.

While magistrates were getting tough on Sunday youngsters arrested 450 and 450 were fined on more offences on the sea front.

Then ordered them to

Back Page

The time,

By MIRROR REPORTER

ON the run they went yesterday—the Mods and Rockers.

A lot of them had ridden into Hastings on their motor scooters and motor bikes on Saturday.

But yesterday many of them were on foot.

And—as these two pictures show—everywhere they went, on the beach or through the town, they were running ... running ... running ...

They ran in the STREETS of this usually quiet seaside town with its old hotels ...

When one of them ran, they all ran. When one of them clapped, they all clapped. When one of them jeered, they all jeered.

The turbulent teen-aged tide seemed sometimes in danger of flooding the normally sedate seaside town. Then the emotional current would change—and sweep on to the BEACH.

There, the crash of scores of feet trampling the shingle drowned the gentle lapping of the tide. And there, at one stage, dozens of youngsters fled before a lone policeman.

ANXIOUS

Crowds milled around aimlessly. Shopkeepers looked on anxiously as the mob swept by.

Hard-pressed police drove round in circles trying to keep up as the Mods changed direction every few minutes, always running ...

But why? No one knows — not even the runners.

ON T

BONK

X164

ONE policem

RDAY. The place, HASTINGS. The tempo, QUICK, very QUICK

E RUN

The Mods and Rockers invade . . but this time it's an 'itchy feet' invasion

s MANY Mods scurrying across the pebbly beach at Hastings yesterday

111

Battle of the Wild Or

Brighton today. Swarms of holidaymakers jam

MONDAY,
AUGUST 3, 1964
THREEPENCE
No. 15054 * *

Daily Herald

IN go the police 'flying squad'

BRITAIN'S HOLIDAY
FLYING SQUAD
STOP A BATTLE
OF HASTINGS

OUT go the Mods and Rockers

BREAK IT UP NOW!

from
**MAX SUICH and
IAN WILLARS**
— HASTINGS, Midnight —

TONIGHT hundreds of teenagers are roaming the front of this Sussex seaside town. A sudden spark—and a savage Clacton-style riot could flare.

Two hours ago 200 Mods suddenly stampeded outside the fashionable Queen's Hotel. Traffic was brought to a standstill by chanting youths and their girls. Four policemen were hustled as they arrested a youth.

KNOCKED OUT

But suddenly the parade of teenagers, moving crocodile-style, swung away. Then, a little later, a policeman was knocked unconscious as he tried to halt a clash between Mods and their Rocker rivals.

The attacked policeman was one of a special squad of 69 flown to Hastings by the RAF this afternoon to stamp out Mod-and-Rocker violence.

SOS CALL

Despite tonight's incidents police from six forces have so far prevented a 1964 Battle of Hastings.

By this morning three thousand Mods and Rockers with their girl friends had swarmed into Hastings, along with the usual Bank Holiday crowds.

Trouble started when Mods and Rockers clashed on the

Into a police car goes a youth on the seafront at Hastings—escorted by three policemen.

ront...and police keep a look-out for trouble.

DAILY Mirror

Monday, August 3, 1964   No. 18,854

RIOT POLICE FLY TO SEASIDE

"Riot squad" police file quietly into the transport plane at Northolt. A few minutes later they were in the air on their way to the trouble town.

orpedo oats ttack U.S. arship

HREE torpedo boats attacked an Ameri-an destroyer 30 miles the coast of Com-unist North Viet-m, in South-East ia, yesterday.

y fired three tor-does, and also at-ked the destroyer ith gunfire

destroyer, Maddox, rd back—and min-es later four jet hters from the merican aircraft car-r Ticonderoga.

Damaged

pokesman in Wash-gton said one of the ats was badly dam-ed and was not oving.

e other two were also maged and "re-ating slowly." American ships and anes were not maged.

r, the US Secretary State, Mr. Dean sk, said that the pedo boats were rth Vietnamese. e other side got a e out of this," he d. "If they do it ain, they'll get an-her sting.

U S is going to use d insist upon using ternational waters." America's Presi-nt Johnson called e advisers to the ite House, appar-tly to discuss the ack

Bombed

included Mr. Rusk d Defence Secre-y Robert Mc-mara

Hanoi, capital of orth Vietnam, a reign Ministry okesman was quoted saying that Ameri-n planes bombed a rder village on turday, wounding person and dam-ing property.

he North Vietnam mmunists are be-ved to be largely hind the guerilla fare now being ged against the erican - backed vernment of South

Then one is beaten up as Mods and Rockers clash

VIOLENCE flared in Hastings last night after Scotland Yard's "Riot Squad" had been flown to the Bank Holiday trouble town.

The police squad who had been standing by at Northolt Airport, near London, were called to the Sussex resort yesterday after noon after a series of skirmishes between Mods and Rockers.

The "Riot Squad," and other reinforcements driven in from nearby holiday towns, had been patrolling Hastings for several hours and had managed to contain the threat-ened violence.

THEN THE CLASH CAME.

One of the London con-stables struggled to arrest a youth involved in a Mods-v.-Rockers scuffle on the sea front.

Blow

He was felled by a blow from behind. For more than a minute he lay stunned on the pavement — as teenagers savagely kicked him.

Then he staggered to his feet and helped pin down a youth.

With four other police, he started carrying the youth to the nearby police station.

Hundreds of screaming youngsters who had been squatting on the beach clattering stones together and screaming rhythmic-ally "Mod! Mod! Mod!" milled around them.

Near the police station there were chants of "Get them"—but suddenly the mob swept off, leaving the

By **JOHN SMITH** and **RONALD RICKETTS**

policemen to carry their prisoner into the police station.

Before the Riot Squad was called to the town, 500-strong crowds of Mods had been on the march disrupt-ing traffic and frightening holidaymakers.

But a special plan drawn up last week when it was learned that Hast-ings was to be "Mod Town" for the Bank Holi-day was put into opera-tion.

The teenagers were met by police at every turn.

And so, until the night clash, there were only two outbreaks of violence.

INCIDENT NO. 1 came when two Rockers were hurled to the ground and kicked savagely after being attacked by Mods near the pier.

INCIDENT NO. 2 came when a seafront cafe owner was slashed on the arm with a broken glass. The wound needed twenty-two stitches.

At least eighteen youths were arrested in skirmishes.

yesterday and last night. They, and three who were charged on Saturday, were brought before a special court which started sitting late in the afternoon.

They faced charges of using threatening be-haviour, causing wilful damage, and damaging police car.

Stones

Inspector Stanley Russell, prosecuting, said of one 16-year-old boy: "He was one of a group of 400 people racing along the foreshore.

"He was seen to throw beach stones."

Another 16-year-old boy was "one of a large group terrorising people on the beach," said the inspector.

All the youths were remanded in custody until tomorrow and were taken to Lewes prison.

MORE TROUBLE be-tween youngsters and police in other seaside towns yesterday. At Brighton two youths and three girls were arrested. Ten youths were held at Great Yarmouth

A constable from Scotland Yard's holiday "Riot Squad" lies stunned on the Hastings promenade as a sergeant from the town force and

another policeman grapple with a youth. The constable had been knocked down and kicked when he tried to make an arrest.

ON THE RUN
— SEE CENTRE PAGES

114

115

Daily Mirror

3d. Tuesday, May 19, 1964 No. 18,789

In two dramatic pictures — all the fury and the hate of the scrap-happy Whitsun Wild Ones

LIVING FOR KICKS

Portrait of a Mod in action at Brighton yesterday

THEY met on the beach at Brighton yesterday—the Mod and the Rocker. And the boot went in . . .

In the picture on the left, the Rocker is lying full-length on the beach.

He was one of a gang of Rockers who fled from a gang of Mods. He tripped and fell. He lay face downwards. Helpless.

There are no rules in the war between Mods and Rockers. And no mercy.

The Mod kicked the Rocker in the face. And when the Rocker (below) was able to lift his head, it was smeared with blood.

This was just one moment of violence out of the many which flared in Brighton and Margate over the Whitsun holiday.

Fines

There was fresh trouble at both resorts yesterday while Sunday's Wild Ones—as reported in Page Four—trooped into court to face the music.

The chairman of Margate magistrates, Dr. George Simpson, made no distinction between Mods and Rockers.

Sawdust Caesars. That was how he described all the young hooligans who turned a holiday into a time of fear and violence.

Fines totalling £1,930 were imposed on forty-five youths at Margate. Thirty-five more were dealt with at Brighton. More will appear in court at both towns today.

The victim, a long-haired Rocker, raises his head after the attack. His face is smeared with blood.

THE BOOT GOES IN

Moment of violence as Mod meets Rocker. The Rocker, lying defenceless, takes a savage kick in the face after falling down on the beach at Brighton.

MORE BATTLES ON THE BEACHES—BACK PAGE

Charge! Mods race to do battle with Rockers. – A handful of holi

ise. They
They can't

DAILY EXPRESS

TUESDAY MAY 19 1964 — No. 19,895   Weather: Sunny   Price 3d.

Mods v. Rockers
battles flare again

These long-haired, mentally unstable petty little sawdust Caesars seem to find courage, like rats, by hunting only in packs . . .
— DR. GEORGE SIMPSON, MARGATE COURT CHAIRMAN, YESTERDAY

COURT REPORT: Page Seven   THE MAGISTRATE: Page Eight

SAWDUST CAESARS

By
RODNEY HALLWORTH, JOHN CLARKE,
and CYRIL AYNSLEY at Margate
GEORGE HUNTER, DANIEL McGEACHIE,
and ROBERT BLACK at Brighton

THERE was Dad asleep in a deckchair and Mum making sandcastles with the children when the 1964 Boys took over the beaches at Margate and Brighton yesterday and smeared the traditional scene with more bloodshed and violence.

In the two towns, magistrates handed out prison sentences and sharp fines to people who were caught on Sunday—and the belt-and-knuckleduster brigade on the sands quietened down.

The final scenes as Whitsun burned itself out was of gangs being chased by police to the railway stations and the Mods and Rockers losing themselves in the convoys home to London.

IN MARGATE trouble began as the railway station with the arrival of the day-trip gangs.

Two hundred boys and girls swarmed into the refreshment room, smashed windows, and tipped tables. The manageress, 53-year-old Mrs. Lily Bull, rushed for the mob.

Two boys threw her. Two more dragged her by the shoulders across the floor.

A cleaner, 50-year-old Mrs. Ellen Green, went to the rescue with a mop. Then—"I was so angry"—she held a door till police arrived.

Knifed

Soon the violence reached the beach, and for Mum and Dad and the children Whitsun ended in terror.

A 20-year-old, Michael Pentico, from Streatham,

In the midst of kicking feet a youth lies on Margate sands unable to escape

**I'll pay
by cheque
boy has
no bank
account**

By TOM MANGOLD

THE boy who said "I'll sign a cheque" when fined £15 at Margate yesterday, admitted last night: "I don't have a bank account.

**Beef price
up again**   **MAKARIOS GOES**   **Triplets
for**

*BUSMA
EDDI
HAS
PROUDE
DAY*

By JIM MI

B US-conducto
Hughes ev
shifts yesterda
started work as
Then, after
finish, he went
from his No. 56
watch Glamorga
the Australians
Cardiff.

He arrived in
see his 22-year
Glyn, a count
hammer the Au
bowlers for 97.
Glyn, a
Cardiff Universi
who goes up to
bridge in O
punched the wic
round the wicke

Caugh

But then, well
a maiden cent
follow his maide
century in w
cricket, he was
swooping silly
The crowd
Eddie among th
to the young bat
he walked a little
unsteady from the
leather in the in
said.

"It was the
You have ne
happening to a
never imagine yo
do it yourself
hardly believe it
He boosted
morgan's score
the highest ind
Australians on t

*Un jeune monde sans morale
a débarqué sur les plages bourgeoises
et effrayé l'Angleterre*

LA TRISTE HISTOIRE DES MODERNS ET DES ROCKERS

500 000 Anglais en bras de chemise et maillot de bain sur les plages de la Manche. C'est le week-end de la Pentecôte. Soudain, 3 000 voyous armés de gourdins, de marteaux à long manche déferlent à travers les transatlantiques. Ce sont deux clans ennemis, le Modern (mod) et le Rocker qui vident une guérilla vieille de deux ans. Il faudra la charge de la police à cheval pour dégager les plages. Bilan : des dizaines de blessés, des centaines d'arrestations et un problème angoissant pour les sociologues britanniques.

REPORTAGE SERGE LEMOINE / ROY DICKENS / MICHAEL HARDY

continued from page 16

got to look even more like the boys,' said Willie Deasey.

The suits they wore had little box jackets and straight skirts. Shiny black patent leather shoes came in. They had either bows on them or various buckles. Long leather coats were smart, or suede ones, often with a leather collar. Coloured leather was used for coats, notably bottle green, navy blue or burgundy, as well as black. Suede coats, which could be three-quarter length, were usually brown with saddle-stitching around the lapels and pocket-flaps, and had covered buttons.

Mods had to be constantly moving. It was important to get around a lot and they took to motor scooters.

The scooter was a British invention but like lots of others, Britain didn't carry it through. I remember one British scooter, the Triumph Tigresse. It was very powerful, and had great acceleration, but it didn't catch on big with Mods. The most popular scooters were the Italian Lambrettas and Vespas. Scooters fitted in with the Mod philosophy. They had smooth lines and were clean and neat. Unlike motorbikes, you didn't get oil on your clothes, or greasy hands.

If a scooter broke down, the super-cool mod wouldn't want to fix it himself. The sight of grease made him go pale. Eddy Grimstead said 'The boys feel it's not a dirty great machine. It's not *working class*, the way the bikes are.' Eddy Grimstead ran two scooter shops in London's East End.

After their initial impact, rising to a peak in 1959, scooter sales dropped. Eddy Grimstead was the first person to realise that scooters hadn't changed at all and decided to make them more exciting. All his scooters were resprayed in unusual colours. Most then had several chrome additions (like the ones on the cover). He became *the* scooter 'customiser'. Apart from the extra lights, mirrors, mascots and horns, he could fit leopard-skin seats, flashy mud-flaps, whip aerials and fur trim around the handlebars.

Kids got very competitive with their scooters as well as their clothes. This could be expensive. The boy on the cover of this book had 27 lamps, 4 Alpine horns, 6 chrome mascots, 4 mirrors and 2 badges. That lot cost him £75 in 1963. Some kids spent up to £200 on extras. When all the lights were on it was amazing, like rows of floodlights. I heard of one scooter Mod who put coloured cellophane in his lamps. He had over 14 different colours when they were lit up.

Kids would cruise down their local High Street in formation. The best scooter would lead and the others would be staggered out behind in an arrow-head shape. There would be anything from 10 to 25 scooters doing about 15 m.p.h. There was a correct way of riding, you stuck your feet out at an angle of 45° and the guy on the pillion-seat held his hands behind his back and lent back. They'd wear Parkas and French berets pulled down over their foreheads. The Parkas were often trimmed with fox fur. Crash helmets were not compulsory at the time.

Other extras included a whole range of silencers. Each one made a different kind of exhaust note. Kids could fly a fox fur from the top of their aerial or let one trail behind in the slipstream. Incredibly long aerials — about 25 feet long — could be obtained. Many of Eddy Grimstead's customised scooters were like works of art. The Royal College of Art's magazine ARK likened Eddy Grimstead to big names in the car *Kustomizing* cult in the States. Lambretta even copied some of his colour schemes.

The in look for scooters changed and scooters loaded with chrome and fox trim suddenly were out. Simpler matt-coloured scooters came in. The accessories were taken off and the tuned silencers discarded as quiet exhausts came back. Some kids went even further and rode around with all the panels off. Their scooters looked like skeletons as though they had been taken off the assembly line before completion. Now not only were the engines exposed (how working class!), but so were the frames and in some cases even the front forks.

It seemed that scooters were bought both as a means of transport and for their importance as cult symbols. Mods were the first group of teenagers to be mobile. You had to get around, to check out other clubs, clothes shops and record shops. You didn't have to worry about getting a late night bus, and, very important, nor did a bird. A boy might spend ages outside the dance hall or Wimpy Bar showing off his machine to other boys, but he was also impressing the birds sitting in the Wimpy Bar looking out. When the time came to pull a bird the scooter had already done half the job.

Groups of scooters used to go to the coast in the summer. Early Saturday mornings you'd see a gaggle of scooters weaving and farting their way down to the sea.

Scooter dealers made it easy for the kids to buy. The deposit was as low as £20 and payments could be extended over three years. They charged higher rates of interest than normal, though. To simplify everything they arranged for Insurance and Road Tax and added it to the weekly payments. This was good salesmanship as it was often very difficult for kids to get their own insurance. The one thing the dealer didn't do was persuade Dad to sign the papers for the hire purchase.

There were many different names associated with Mod. All names came, like the fashions, from the Mods themselves, not from anyone outside. The hierarchy contains the following ranks: Modernists, Mods, Faces, Stylists, Individualists, Numbers, Tickets, Mids, Mockers, Seven and Sixes, States, Moddy Boys and Scooter Boys. There were probably others that I never came across.

Modernists were the earliest Mods. The forerunners of the style. 'Mods' is the term that covers the whole spectrum of different types. A 'Face' was a top Mod, a fashion leader that the younger Mods, the

Moddy Boys, would try to copy. If somebody initiated a new look, he'd be a Face. The first guys to wear plimsoles down the Scene, or to dance a certain way would also be Faces. There was a little secret society of Mods that began their weekend at *Ready Steady Go* studios on a Friday, and shopped and dance 'Up West' through to Sunday night. These were mostly Faces and they would go back to their own neighbourhood in the week and be Top Mod in their local dance hall.

The world in which Mods existed was a changing, shifting place and the styles changed. What the Faces were wearing in 1963, the others were wearing in 1964, and the Faces wouldn't be seen in. They were always striving to be new and one jump ahead. The names they called themselves changed and shifted too as things evolved. Faces stopped calling themselves Mods towards the latter part of 1964, mostly because of the riots but also because the newer kids were different and the Faces disapproved. They called themselves 'Individualists', or 'Stylists'. They wanted to differentiate themselves from the over-all uniformity they saw in the suburban and provincial Mod.

The kids were called 'Numbers' or 'Tickets' or 'Seven and Sixes' by the older, more established Faces. There might have been differences between these terms. I heard them all mentioned at various times, but no one ever defined the terms, and they won't be in any dictionary. They were made up on the spot, in the streets, by no one in particular and spread by word of mouth.

I think the term 'Numbers' referred to the numbers the younger Mods wore on their T-shirts. 'Seven and Sixes' were called that because they wore T-shirts from Woolworths that cost 7/6d.

The 'States' were the kids that thought they were Mods because they wore a pair of Levis and a British Home Stores brand of Fred Perry. They went along with the pack but didn't have a clue how Mods looked really. They were very half-hearted about it all. Girls who tagged along but didn't have the right idea were called 'States'. Literally they looked a 'bit of a state' to other Mods.

'Mockers' were kids who didn't fit into the styles of Mods *or* Rockers. To a lot of people there were only two choices. You were either a Mod or a Rocker. There was nothing else. 'Mockers' wore Rocker-style clothes only as a fashion, not for the practical reasons Rockers had. They would wear the leather-style motor-cycle jackets of the Rockers, only theirs were made of nylon. They would have Mod haircuts.

'Mids' were similar to 'Mockers' (confusing isn't it?) The 'Mockers' dress borrowed bits from both Mods and Rockers. They did so intentionally. 'Mids' did the same but didn't realise it. They would wear a Madras jacket over a white T-shirt with their initials on, and Levis, but have on black winklepickers and a Beatle style haircut.

The only thing kids would stay in for, was *Ready, Steady, Go* on I.T.V., on Friday evenings. Parents used to be 'glued' to the telly. Mods might watch *The Man From U.N.C.L.E.* but not much else. *R.S.G.*. was *the* Mods show. At about seven minutes past six on a Friday evening, the *R.S.G.* Op-art graphic credits would appear and thousands of Mods all over the country would feel that rush of excitement once again. '5,4,3,2,1 The weekend starts here!'

For Johnny Moke and Willie Deasey, the weekend would have already started, because they danced every week on *R.S.G.* and had to be there in the afternoon for a rehearsal. The dancers used to be chosen every week from the Scene or some other London club.

Theresa Confrey and Patrick Kerr were the full time dancers who demonstrated new dances for *R.S.G.*. Theresa and Patrick were like professional mods to the media along with people like the Dave Clarke Five (for whom Mods had nothing but contempt) and Cathy McGowan.

Cathy McGowan used to present *R.S.G.*. She was selected because she was simply a typical suburban teenager. She fluffed her lines and said everything was 'super' and 'terrific'. But at least she wasn't a patronising professional and despite her faults, or because of them, Mods liked her and accepted her. *R.S.G.* had its token boring old fart presenter in the middle-aged Keith Fordyce. Michael Aldred and Gay Singleton interviewed the stars and guests. For those who went to dance on *R.S.G.* there was a warm-up man called Paul Raven (he later called himself Gary Glitter and became a seventies teenyboppers star). Patrick and Theresa would visit the Scene club, not only to pick dancers but also to find out the latest dances. *R.S.G.* presented a new dance every week. It was the way the rest of the country kept up with the West End.

Johnny Moke explains, 'They'd see a new dance, although sometimes it was just a heel flick or something that was different like an arm movement. We'd show them it and teach them the steps at rehearsals. They'd give it a name, usually something really silly, and show it that week. They might link it to a new record and give it the name of the record.'

No music show on T.V. has since captured anything like the sheer excitement and hectic pace of *R.S.G.*. It did away with all the razmatazz of previous pop shows. It was probably the chaos and informality of having the audience part of the show, getting pushed out of the way by cameras and dancing around the cables and bumping into Andrew Oldham or Diana Ross.

It was possible to see the groups you actually *wanted* to see, instead of what 'they' wanted you to see, like Frank Ifield, Ken Dodd or Susan Maughan. *R.S.G.* would have the American artistes like The Miracles, James Brown, Dionne Warwick, Inez and Charlie Foxx, Little Stevie Wonder, The Supremes, Ike and Tina Turner and Otis Reding. From England they'd have the Beatles, the Stones, the Animals, the

Who, and nearly every important group, big or small. It was all very fast moving, so even if a programme did include Tom Jones, Dave Clark and Cliff Richard, it wasn't long before another act appeared.

R.S.G. would fly acts over from the States. It was worth it for a lot of American artists to visit England to do *R.S.G.* because they were bigger in England than they were in the States. I remember seeing Jimmy Reed once at the Flamingo. He didn't have any idea what was going on. There he was, trying to make his living out of putting his suffering to music, and suddenly he's flown out of his country to Europe to play to rich white kids all pilled out of their minds and treating him like the Messiah. He was standing there playing his guitar looking very bewildered, with his manager next to him, both still in their overcoats and scarves.

R.S.G. had a number of specials too. They had a Beatles special, and a Stones special, one for the Who and I think one for Otis Redding or James Brown. The London based bands became almost regulars, such as The Who, Animals and Stones. People like Mick Jagger and Kenny Lynch always happened to be passing by and would pop in.

Not only did *R.S.G.* keep Mods up to date on dances, but it also had on some of the best-dressed Mods every week, so the rest of the country saw something of London Mods clothes. Some kids were very influenced by the fashions they saw on *R.S.G.*. Paul Beecham was one of the dancers from the Scene who was regularly on the programme. It is said that he was one of the originators of the 'Block'. He used to appear wearing jeans with small turn-ups, hockey-boots with the studs removed, and a cycling shirt. He was on for six weeks and then was ill. A couple of weeks later while still ill he watched the show and saw a kid dancing in exactly the same clothes he'd worn. 'The guy even copied my watch-strap and the way I wore my watch with the face on the inside of the wrist.'

Johnny Moke recalls one particular show: 'Sandie Shaw was on the show and it was her first T.V. appearance. She had to walk along a bit and go up three steps. She couldn't see very well without her glasses, so somebody, I think it was one of the technicians, suggested she took her shoes off and felt along the cable with her feet up to the steps. She did and got known for being the barefoot singer.'

The signature tune opening *R.S.G.* was a current hit from the time and was changed about every six months. The most apt was *Anyway, Anyhow, Anywhere* by the Who. The record has always seemed to me to be about a typical 'pilled up' Mod. It might not, I've never heard Pete Townshend talk about the song. It could just as easily be about his new found wealth or the state of his ego at that time.

I can go anyway, way I choose,
I can live anyhow, win or lose,
I can go anywhere for something new,
Anywhere, anyhow, anyway I choose.

I can do anything, right or wrong;
I can talk anyhow to get along.
I don't care anyway, I never lose,
Anyway, anyhow, anywhere I choose.

The two essentials that a full time Soho Mod needed in the Sixties to keep him on the go were money and energy. Most Mods were in a clean clerical job that was relatively well paid. There wasn't a large unemployment problem for school leavers then. If they didn't have the money they wouldn't try to be in the competitive top league. They would improvise and get by. I know of kids that would stay indoors for weeks until they'd saved enough to buy whatever it was that they found they weren't able to live without. Rather than be seen not looking right, it was better not to be seen.

In order to keep up the hectic pace that was expected of the true Mod, he would have to supplement his energy. The true Mod was half real and half myth. The itinerary of our ideal Mod went like this. Monday evening, The Scene Club. Tuesday, local dance. Wednesday, La Discothèque. Thursday, The Scene again or maybe the Marquee or the Lyceum. Friday, *Ready, Steady, Go* and then on to the Scene or La Discothèque. Saturday, shopping down Carnaby Street in the morning, then to Imhoff's or some obscure record shop in Hampstead or Brixton. Saturday night to the Flamingo and Allnighter. Leave the Allnighter at four in the morning and go to a Sunday morning street-market like Petticoat Lane or Brick Lane for tea and breakfast and to browse among the record and clothes stalls. Sunday afternoon back to the Flamingo for the afternoon session. Sunday evening to the Crawdaddy club in Richmond, ending up for a *cappuccino* at L'Auberge coffee bar by Richmond Bridge until midnight.

Somewhere in all that he'd have to fit in washing his hair and a little time to listen to the records he'd bought. Even if this was the Mod myth, many Mods kept up a lifestyle almost as hectic as this. Most were broke by Monday morning but could still keep going. Johnny Moke: 'All you needed was about 1/- for fares, 6d there and 6d back. It was two bob to get in the Lyceum or Tottenham Royal. I didn't drink or smoke, I might buy an orange drink which was 6d. All we wanted to do was dance.'

In order to get the energy for this activity Mods took purple hearts. Purple Hearts were tablets called Drynamil shaped like a curved triangle and purply blue in colour. Doctors prescribed them for 'anxiety'. The dose would be one tablet. Mods took two, three, five, then fourteen or even more. If you took half a dozen 'hearts' you felt like you could 'Go anywhere, live anyhow and go anyway . . .'

It gave kids the artificial energy needed to dance non-stop throughout the night. It also gave them the 'bottle' to steal and shoplift the clothes they couldn't really afford. Now they had the energy to go dancing a lot more, they needed more clothes.

The purple hearts also fed the Mod myth. Kids would exaggerate about everything. About how much their shoes were, and when they were getting their new scooter, how many girls they'd had, and how many pills they'd taken. They would end up believing their own lies.

The Ticket living in some dreary suburb, sitting in the Wimpy trying to make his cheeseburger last all night staring out at the rain was still part of the Mod myth. He was *going* to get a chromed scooter and five suits in Tonik or ice-blue Mohair, and have some basketweave shoes hand made, and get his hair styled in Wardour Street and go dancing in the West End clubs every night. He was a Mod. He had his stake in the Myth.

Pills made you think you were living life to the full. You certainly were doing something every minute you were 'blocked'. You had no choice. You couldn't keep still. There was so much artificial energy running through you that you had to keep moving. The pills not only relieved anxiety, they would induce intense euphoria. Your heart would beat much faster and your pupils enlarge. Your brain would race and you'd try to say all the things going through your brain, only it was impossible to say it all fast enough.

The best story I know to sum up this aspect of being blocked came from Jack English, a Mod from Leicester. 'This friend of mine was very blocked up, talking away like crazy. We were in a flat on the second floor and he was sitting out on the balcony railings facing in, talking to us. He was so involved in conversation that he forgot where he was, leaned over backwards and fell off the balcony. We all rushed downstairs and when we got to him he was still talking away like mad. He didn't realise he'd fallen off the balcony.'

Irish Jack, who was a Mod from Shepherds Bush, invented the term 'Chewing gum weekends'. This was because of the habit of constantly chewing because you had to have something to use up your energy. If you didn't chew chewing gum, the danger was that you would chew your own gum. After a 'chewing gum weekend', the jaw muscles ached. Mind you, so did everything else, so the sore jaw didn't stand out too much.

After a while the makers of purple hearts announced they were changing the pills. There had been a lot of comment in parliament about the pill-pushing business, and lurid headlines appeared in the press like 'SCOOTER BOY WAS A PURPLE HEART DRUNK!' There were huge sums of money being made from supplying purple hearts. Every club had at least one person who was selling pills. They were 6d each. They used to come in little brown envelopes with a little cellophane window at the front, or in wage packets. I knew somebody who thought the little envelopes were made especially for packing pills. He used to ask for two packets of pill envelopes in his local stationers. There were bigger pushers who supplied the kids that sold in the clubs.

The Home Secretary, Henry Brooke, went on a tour of the Soho clubs accompanied by plain clothes detectives. 'What I saw,' he said afterwards, 'convinced me something should be done about the drug peddlars.' He proposed a maximum fine of £200 or six months imprisonment for possession. Purple hearts immediately went up to 9d each. But there was still no shortage. So the makers of Drynamil said they'd take the purple and the heart out of them. They'd change them and keep the colour and shape of the new ones a secret.

As soon as purple hearts disappeared new kinds of amphetamines appeared. French blues, dexedrine and black bombers all hit the clubs. 'Blues' were light blue with a line down the middle and supposed to be double the strength of the old purple hearts. 'Black Bombers' were black capsules and very strong. Lots of kids wouldn't touch them. They were about 2/- each and probably damaged many a brain. 'Dexes' were yellow and cost a shilling.

Kids were getting silly and swallowing anything. The trouble with pills or 'speed' or 'dubes' or 'leapers' or whatever names they had, was that all that incredible dynamism and boundless euphoria had to be paid for. Kids thought they were indestructable. What they didn't realise was that you couldn't 'get nothing for nothing'. What was gained on the swings had to be paid for on the roundabouts. The roundabouts were usually Monday mornings. The 'come down' was very unpleasant. When the pills effect wore off, it was realised that the body, which had been taken beyond its natural limitations, actually had muscles and joints, and that every one of them was sore and throbbing with pain. Worse than that was 'the horrors': terrible depression and fearful hallucinations. The constant use of leapers really showed with some kids. They looked liked walking skulls. Their eyes sunk deep in their sockets and their hollow cheeks. The worst damage the pills did was psychological not physical. There were many victims around suffering from paranoia and schizophrenia.

One trouble with taking pills was that you were never quite sure how many you'd taken. So to be on the safe side you took a few more. Johnny Moke tells of a friend of his called Scruffy Pete. 'He was found outside the Flamingo in Wardour Street collapsed on the pavement. They rushed him to hospital and pumped out his stomach and found he'd taken 76 purple hearts. He'd just kept taking more, and forgetting, and taking still more. He survived that time. No wonder painted on the wall at the back of the Marquee in two foot letters was, SPEED KILLS.'

Pills certainly used to get you 'hung up' over things. There was a kid on the beach at Brighton on his hands and knees searching among the pebbles and muttering, 'I must find that half, I've gotta find that half.' He was seen still around the same spot four hours later, trying to find half a pill he'd dropped.

There was another kid at Brighton with a shoe box full of all kinds of pills and capsules selling them quite openly. The Mod girls used to carry the pills for the boys because the police didn't stop the girls much.

There were small clubs and cafés set up exclusively for pill-pushing. In one East London café, you could get tea 'with' or 'without'. 'Without' was 5d and 'with' was 2/5d, for which you got two pills in the tea.

Buying pills could be very sordid. I once went to a dingy club in a shop's premises in Shepherds Bush Road. It was very seedy. We sat with a cardboard-burger and a cup of froth while the waiter went off to get 'our order', which took about 15 minutes. No wonder an M.P. called these dives 'Pig Bins with juke boxes'.

Laurie Conway from Enfield was at the Scene club when it was raided. 'Suddenly the floor was covered in pills. The toilets were blocked (sic) with leapers. Kids were kicking pills away from them along the floor so there weren't any near where they were standing. Everybody was searched and questioned. They had about five Inspector-types and some kids were arrested and taken upstairs. There were police vans lined up all down the road.' The pill craze died down a bit, early in 1965. It was affluence and this artificial energy that had been fuelling the most active Mods, especially the ones who just wanted to dance all through the weekends.

Up until the Twist, dancers had been in couples. The Twist was the first dance where the partners danced separately. It caught on everywhere. It brought exhibitionism and sex-display to the fore. It also brought competition between the partners. The boy could outdance the girl, or vice versa. Sweet old-fashioned romance gave way to fun, exhibitionism and competitiveness. Other dance crazes followed. The Hully Gully, the Monkey, the Turkey Trot, the Madison, the Locomotion, the Fly and Mashed Potato. Most originated in the States and had a hit record associated with them.

In 1962 Mods evolved their own dances. The first was the Shake. It was also called the Blues or the French Blues and varied from club to club. It was the basic dance from which endless others were derived. After the Shake boys and girls didn't necessarily dance together. You could dance on your own, with a group of your own sex, or with the opposite sex. Eventually the best dances to appear were the Block and the Bang. These dances were very tight and fast and neat. The tightness was partly because in a crowded club you only had a tiny patch of floor to dance in. In the Bang, the dancer moved sideways across the floor in a crab-like movement. In the Block, the footwork was very fast and intricate and involved swaying and balancing on the tips of the heels. Not many could perfect the Block.

Every week a new dance would appear. Johnny Moke gives a reason for this: 'If you dance all night, say

for five hours, you've easily mastered the latest dance and you improvise because you're so bloody bored doing it the same way. You think, "That was a great step, I'll work on that one." You're already creating a new dance.' Kids would practise in front of a mirror at home before trying a new dance in public. Dancing was so important to many Mods it had to be perfect.

The dance hall was very significant. It was where they lived. Kids expressed themselves through their clothes and their dancing. Johnny Moke said, 'You didn't want to be like Joe Bloggins on the factory line. The working class were making it. John Stephen, David Bailey, Mick Jagger, Terence Stamp, The Beatles were all very young and working class and were very successful. The social barriers were down. We all thought we were going to make it. In the dance hall, you could *be* somebody.'

Some dances were plain gimmicky, like the Loco-motion, where you make the motions of a steam engine. The Shimmy was a dance where you shook all over 'just like a jelly on a plate'. 'Later on, the record industry tried to get in on the act and launched commercially contrived dances like the Loddy-Lo and the Carnaby, but nobody took any notice and they didn't catch on.''

Blue Beat records and the dances associated with them did catch on. They came from the Roaring Twenties club which was a West Indian club in, of all places, Carnaby Street. It was nearly all Jamaicans and very dark and heavy with pot smoke. The music was deafening and you couldn't see much but teeth and eyes, but the dancing and records were fantastic. *Blue Beat* and *Melodisc* were the original Sky record labels run by Ziggy Jackson. He had Prince Buster on his label.

Most people who look back on the sixties Mods scene remember it as a battle between Mods and Rockers. This was because that was the aspect of it presented in the press. Actually there wasn't constant hostility between the two groups. They didn't like each other. Mods thought Rockers were greasy, scruffy, uncouth, out of date, crude and boring idiots. A bunch of leather-clad louts and layabouts. Rockers thought Mods were weedy, dressed up, stuck up, cissified, poncey and effeminate nancies. A bunch of prissy little jerks.

They didn't, however, waste a lot of time abusing each other or fighting. In lots of places (including London) there were mostly Mods. In the rural areas and more Northern Towns there were mostly Rockers. So they didn't bump into each other too much. I know of Mods that lived in predominantly Rocker areas, and they had to be constantly on the lookout so as not to run into a bunch of Rockers. Ric, who was a Mod in Wembley, moved to East Grinstead — Rocker country. 'I didn't see all that much of them at first because I used to go and stay with friends in London every weekend. If you did have to walk past a group of Rockers, you'd think, "Oh no, here it comes." Not any violence, just plenty of verbal, taking the mickey. It could get really tedious and embarrassing. I'd always check a train carriage before I got in to see if it held a bunch of Rockers.'

My own strongest memory of Mods was how gentle they were. When I was running a Mod club they were incredibly helpful and friendly. Not aggressive or loutish at all. Even when there was some aggression, they were reasonable. One day the Harrow Mods were 'gonna get the Greenford Mods', because somebody had danced with Vespa Vince's girl. I was told about it and I passed word back through the club grapevine that if there was a fight the club could be closed. The two area leaders appeared looking very concerned. 'We don't want any trouble for the club. We'll beat hell out of each other at some later date, somewhere that won't get the club closed.' We all ended up having a drink together and talking about the group that was playing.

The press reports of the Clacton riots changed a lot of things. After Clacton, Mods and Rockers were suddenly seen as violent hoodlums. Neither side was. There were a few idiots and trouble-makers at Clacton, not much to do, and not much else to fill the newspapers with.

Word had gone round the coffee bars and Mod clubs that everyone was going to Clacton. They weren't going for a fight, they often went to the coast for a weekend. So when the Easter Bank Holiday weekend came hundreds of Mods poured into Clacton. Clacton was a small resort and not particularly affluent. It didn't have too many amenities and certainly not enough to keep all those kids entertained. The weather was also the worst for ages. The Easter Sunday was the coldest since 1884. The main problem was boredom. On a hot sunny day it would have been all right, but as the weather was bad, the kids found too little to do. Lots of cafés and places weren't open because their season had not yet begun. The ones that were open were often refusing to serve the kids, who were probably making a nuisance of themselves.

Johnny Moke and Willie Deasey were at Clacton. 'When the pubs closed after lunchtime, there was nothing to do. Kids were just milling around. We went down to the pier. It was 1/- to get on, so a lot of us jumped over the turnstyle. Then for a laugh some kids went up the helter-skelter the wrong way. It was stupid but just a lark really. The police came and everybody started running. Some old ladies got pushed out of the way. I think that's called a riot. Kids began to congregate in bigger crowds. They nicked Easter eggs and stuff from the shops. That evening it was on the news and next day it was ridiculous.'

The news of the trouble at Clacton resulted in hundreds more Mods making their way towards the small resort. Also holidaymakers went along to see the 'troubles'. Cameramen and reporters turned up. The following day, the kids were expected to do something. Willie says, 'A lot of kids looking for trouble came on the second day. We were all standing in a crowd when everybody started throwing things. Our mate Mickey Butler got hit on the head by a newspaper stand. He was just standing there, and it came flying through the air and hit him on the head.'

Shops were damaged and there was some scuffling with the police. A few Rockers happened to be in Clacton and were involved but it wasn't a Mod versus Rocker battle. More likely, London Mods versus local shopkeepers and police. The press exaggerated the trouble. The Daily Telegraph reported, 'DAY OF TERROR BY SCOOTER GROUPS'. The Mirror front page read, 'SCOOTER GANGS "BEAT UP" CLACTON', and WILD ONES INVADE SEASIDE — 97 ARRESTS'. Every national newspaper except the Times had the 'Clacton Affair' on the front pages. The story ran on both the Monday and Tuesday. The papers were full of words like, *terror, frenzy, rampaging* and *running amok*. There weren't any major news stories that weekend, so Clacton got the full treatment.

A very sensible article appeared in the *East Essex Gazette*, the local paper that covered Clacton. 'The troubles . . . were not so horrific as the flood of national press, television and radio publicity suggested. The town was not wrecked, no one, apart from some of the young hooligans themselves, was really hurt, and Clacton housewives certainly did not, as one early morning broadcaster said, spend Tuesday "sweeping up the glass from their broken windows".'

An assistant editor of one of the national dailies admitted afterwards that it had been 'a little over-reported.' But the press now devoted lots of space to trying to understand Mods and Rockers. The names were almost inseparable, as though a new media term like 'Dolly Bird' had been added to their vocabulary — 'Modsnrockers'. The 'Modsnrockers' were analysed, advised, warned, feared, and fussed over.

The press, without actually saying so, were building up for the next confrontation. Clacton had been first, which town was to be next? Not everyone lost their heads over it. I particularly liked Lord Arran's comment in the Evening News of April 1st 1964 . . . 'I am truly sorry for Clacton — a nice warm-hearted place. If some town had to cop it, I would have preferred Frinton. They are snooty at Frinton.'

The next Bank Holiday was Whitsun. This time there *was* trouble between the Mods and the Rockers. Clacton stood by for an invasion but hardly anyone went there. The main troublespots were Brighton, Margate and Bournemouth. There were also small incidents in other places like the fairground at Hampstead Heath in London. The police had a difficult job in Brighton and Margate, but in lots of cases they missed the real troublemakers and arrested the nearest likely-looking kid as a token gesture to law and order. The scene had been set for a battle. People had gone down to see the skirmishes. After all it was cheaper than taking the children to the circus. The press were standing around with cameras waiting for something to happen. This time it couldn't be put down to boredom due to bad weather — the Whitsun weather was fine and sunny. There were now groups of demented, pilled-up yobs dressed as Mods and Rockers and they wanted trouble.

The Magistrates at Margate and Hastings had had as much as they could take after the riots. At Margate, the chairman of the magistrates said, 'These long-haired, unkempt, mentally unstable, petty little sawdust Caesars can only find courage by hunting in packs like rats.' A Daily Mail reporter stated, 'They're pin-neat, lively and clean, but a rat-pack.' They were also called vermin and show-offs.

After the second wave of violence, the top Mods began to dissociate themselves from the hooligan element. True Mods were really too concerned for their clothes to want to ruin them by fighting with worthless Rockers. The smoother Mods disapproved of the fighting and thought the others were really Rockers in Mods clothing. They stopped calling themselves Mods and carried on as before as Stylists.

1964 and 1965 were the peak of the Mod look and in many ways they were the best. But if the riots had sown the seeds of the end of the look, the harder, newer Mods finished it off. The riots became a regular event every bank holiday. At the August Bank Holiday of 1964, the kids went to Hastings but the police flew in reserves and kept the kids moving around the town until they got fed up and went home.

By the middle of 1966 the scene had widened and opened out and changed drastically. The Scene had closed; *Ready, Steady, Go* had finished and the kids had got bored with rioting at the seaside. Carnaby Street had gone Disney and commercial Mod clubs like Tiles were opening.

By now, the Mods had their own, English, groups to identify with. The main two were the Who and the Small Faces. In 1965 the Who had released a staggeringly good serious rock anthem about Mods called *My Generation*. Pete Meaden was still 100% hip and 100% mod, and travelling around with his new band, Jimmy James and the Vagabonds.

But the rest of the world had caught up. Bob Dylan, The Beatles, the Stones and the Beach Boys had all progressed rapidly. The atmosphere generally was very healthy. The conditions that existed at the beginning of the Sixties had altered. Radio was playing the stuff the kids wanted to hear. Shops were selling the stuff kids wanted to buy. Kids weren't dancing so much now, they were listening and talking about 'Love'. If you turned off your mind and floated downstream you didn't particularly want to dance as well.

Credits to Pictures

5   Photo by Bob Freeman from *The Sunday Times Colour Magazine* article on Mods, 'Changing Faces' published August 2nd 1964.
17   Top pic. Carnaby St., June 1964. *Colorific*. Lower pic. Carnaby St., 1964. *Popperfoto*.
18   *Hairdressers Journal* 1963.
19   *Evening News* 22nd May 1964. *Associated Newspaper Group Ltd.*
20   Steve Marriot, Roger Daltrey and Ronnie Lane by courtesy of *Fabulous* magazine. Rod Stewart, *Rex Features*.
21   Top pic. Carnaby St. looking in window of 'Mod Male'. *Colorific* July 1964. Desert boot courtesy of *Clarks Shoes*. Drawing courtesy of *Hairdressers Journal* 1964.
22, 23   Sixties clothes by courtesy of *Contemporary Wardrobe*.
24, 25   Carnaby St. July 1964. *Colorific*.
26   Top left, Carnaby St. 1964 *Popperfoto*. Bottom right, Carnaby St., June 1964 *Colorific*. Roger Daltrey and Pete Townshend in Carnaby St., courtesy *Fabulous* magazine.
27   John Stephens Man's shop, Carnaby St. 1964, both *Colorific*.
28, 29   Two girls in Carnaby St. 1962 *Camera Press*. Series of pics. in 'Mod Male', Carnaby St., July 1964, *Colorific*. Daily Mail Sept. 15 1964., *Associated Newspaper Group Ltd.*
30, 31, 32   *Hairdressers Journal* Magazine Section, July 1965.
33   *Hairdressers Journal* Magazine Section, October 1963.
34   Top pic. Mods leaving club in Putney, July 1964. Lower pic. of Mods in light coloured suits (and face powder) 1964, Both *Colorific*.
35   Inside dance hall in Putney July 1964, *Colorific*.
36   Both pics. of Cockney Scooter Club 1964, *Colorific*.
37   Top Pic. Scooter Mods, Clacton 1964, *Keystone*. Lower pic. Brighton May 1964, *Colorific*.
38   Young Mod girls dancing. September 1963, *Syndication International*.
39   Scooter Mod at Margate June 1964, *Syndication International*.
40, 41   Ready, Steady, Go session. August 1964, *Colorific*.
43   Top pic. Cathy McGowan and Kenny Lynch on R.S.G., *Camera Press*. Lower Pic. Dancers demonstrating 'The Fox' on R.S.G. Patrick Kerr on right, *Colorific*.
44   Top pic. Hastings 1964, *Colorific*. Lower pic. The Who at Brighton, *Fabulous* magazine.
45   Hastings August 1964, *Colorific*.
46, 47   May 1964, *Syndication International*.
48   Top pic. Brighton June 1964, *Colorific*. Lower pic. Margate June 1964, *Syndication International*.
49   Margate June 1964, *Syndication International*.
50   Hastings August 1964, *Colorific*.
51   Top pic. July 1964, *Rex Features*. Lower pic. Brighton July 1964, *Colorific*.
52   Top left, 'Scene' club January 1964, *Rex Features*. Top right and lower pic, November 1963, *Syndication International*.
53   Brighton July 1964, *Syndication International*.
54, 55   Some Mod dances. Arranged by Johnny Moke.
56, 57   Brighton 1964, *Syndication International*.
58   Top pic. Hastings August 1964, Lower pic. Brighton May 1964, Both *Colorific*.
59   Top pic. Hastings August 1964, *Syndication International*. Lower pic. Hastings August 1964, *Colorific*.
60, 61   All pics at Hastings August 1964, All *Syndication International*.
62, 63   Hastings 1964, *Syndication International*.
64, 65   Brighton May 1964, Both *Colorific*.
66   Both pics. Brighton May 1964, Both *Syndication International*.
67   Top pic. Hastings August 1964, *Colorific*. Lower pic. Hastings August 1964, *Keystone*.
68   Top left and bottom left pics. Brighton May 1964, Both *Syndication International*. Top right pic. June 1964, *Colorific*. Lower right pic. November 1963, *Syndication International*.

69   Hastings August 1964, *Syndication International*.
70, 71   Hastings August 1964, *Syndication International*.
72   Margate May 1964, *Press Association/Reuter*.
73   Hastings 1964, *Syndication International*.
76, 77   Mickey Tenner and Sandy Sarjeant at the 'Scene' club June 1964, *Colorific*.
79   Top pic. Kinks rehearse for R.S.G. 1964, *Rex Features*. Lower left, Jimmy Reed on R.S.G., *Rex Features*. Lower right, High Numbers in 1964, *Fabulous* magazine.
82   Pic. by Bob Freeman from *Sunday Times Colour Magazine* article on Mods, 'Changing Faces' published August 2nd. 1964.
83   September 1965, *Syndication International*.
84, 85   All *Colorific*.
86   Brighton 1964, *Colorific*.
87   Pic. same as cover by Ian Maitland. May 1964, *Syndication International*. (First appeared in Daily Mirror).
88   Lambretta factory. *Syndication International*.
89   Lower pic. Brighton May 1964, *Colorific*.
90   Daily Mirror, May 23rd. 1964, *Syndication International*.
91   Top pic. Margate June 1964, *Syndication International*. Lower pic. 1964, *Syndication International*.
92   Sunday Mirror, 1964, *Syndication International*.
93   Poster outside 'La Discothèque' 1963, *Popperfoto*.
94, 95   Sunday Mirror, 1964, *Syndication International*.
96, 97   Inside and outside the 'Scene' club. 1963, *Popperfoto*.
98   Top pic. Outside 'La Discothèque' 1963, *Popperfoto*. Lower pic. Dance Hall in Putney 1964, *Colorific*.
99   'Scene' club, July 1964, *Colorific*. (Pete Meaden in centre).
100, 101   The 'High Numbers' dancing the 'Block' at the 'Scene' club, July 1964, *Colorific*.
102, 103   Mods dancing at 'Scene' club. Coloured Singer with 'High Numbers' is Ronnie Jones, July 1964, *Colorific*.
104, 105   The 'High Numbers' play 'Gotta Dance to Keep From Crying', at 'Scene' club, July 1964, *Colorific*.
106, 107   Pic. of Brighton Beach, Whit Sunday 1964, from Daily Mail, *Associated Newspaper Group Ltd.*
108, 109   Margate Beach, Whit Sunday 1964, *Keystone*.
110   Daily Mirror, March 30th 1964, *Syndication International*. Daily Sketch, May 19th 1964, *Associated Newspaper Group Ltd.*
111   Daily Mirror, August 3rd 1964, *Syndication International*.
112   Daily Herald, August 3rd 1964, *Syndication International*. Long pic. from Evening Standard, May 18th 1964, *London Express News and Features*.
113   Pic. of fighting, Hastings, August 1964, *Colorific*.
114   Daily Mirror, August 3rd 1964, *Syndication International*.
115   Both pics., Hastings August 1964, *Colorific*.
116   Daily Mirror, May 19th 1964, *Syndication International*.
117   Both pics., Hastings August 1964, *Colorific*.
118   Series of pics., Brighton May 1964, *Syndication International*. Daily Express, May 19th 1964, *London Express News and Feature Services*. Pic. of Margate Beach from Daily Mirror May 18th 1964, *Syndication International*.
119   Two pages from *Paris Match* published May 30th 1964.
120, 121   Brighton, Whit Monday 1964, *Press Association/Reuter*.

The publishers wish to give thanks to Pete Townshend for permission to reprint part of Anyway, Anyhow, Anywhere, by Peter Townshend and Roger Daltrey, first published in 1966 by Fabulous Music.